SŌKA GAKKAI, BUILDERS OF THE THIRD CIVILIZATION

*American
and Japanese Members*

SŌKA GAKKAI, BUILDERS OF THE THIRD CIVILIZATION

American and Japanese

Members

BY

James Allen Dator

University of Washington Press

Seattle & London

Copyright © 1969 by the University of Washington Press
Library of Congress Catalog Card Number 68–8509
Manufactured by the Colonial Press Inc., Clinton, Mass.
Printed in the United States of America
DESIGNED BY KLAUS GEMMING

TO TISH

PREFACE

THIS STUDY dates from the fall of 1962 when a young man and a young woman came to my house on the campus of Rikkyō University in Tokyo, Japan, and asked if they could speak with me. They came into my study and sat together in front of me. Without any explanation of who they were or what they wanted, they directly asked me, in Japanese, "What is the purpose of religion?" My questioners, I soon discovered, were members of the Sōka Gakkai,[1] and the purpose of their visit was to effect my conversion to Nichiren Shōshū, the religion of which Sōka Gakkai is a lay organization. Why they decided to come to me, a foreigner, teaching political science in the College of Law and Politics of a university whose chairman of the board of trustees is the archbishop of the Japanese Episcopal Church (Nippon Seikōkai), I never found out, but through my association with them I was for several months able to attend meetings, engage in discussions with various leaders and ordinary members, and receive considerable printed matter as a potential convert. When it finally became evident that I was not going to convert, they eventually gave up and departed with the words: "That's all right. You don't have to join now, although you will miss many divine benefits and suffer much hardship because you are resisting. But you will convert sometime. Nichiren Daishōnin will win!"

As a result of this experience, for the remaining four of my six years in Japan I engaged in systematic research into the Sōka Gakkai. My interests have been primarily sociological and political, not theological or philosophical. I have sought answers to such questions as: What is the social function of the Sōka Gakkai? What kinds of people become members of the Sōka Gakkai, and why do they join? How are Sōka Gakkai members different from persons who are not members? What are the

[1] Also commonly transliterated in English as one word, "Sōkagakkai."

political and social principles, aims, and methods of the Sōka Gakkai?

In order to answer these questions, I have used five types of research:

1. Participant observation. I had only a brief direct encounter with ordinary members of the Sōka Gakkai, but my major research collaborator, Mr. Koichi Niitsu of the Department of Sociology of Rikkyō University and a specialist on acculturation, became a member of an American chapter of the Sōka Gakkai at Yokosuka (near Yokohama) and accumulated nearly twenty hours of taped recordings of both American and Japanese Sōka Gakkai meetings, in addition to having valuable first-hand contact with American and Japanese members.

2. Analysis of material published by the Sōka Gakkai. I have subscribed to, accumulated, and analyzed most major publications of the Sōka Gakkai since 1960, and selected materials before that date. These are cited in the Bibliography.

3. Analysis of material about the Sōka Gakkai. These are also listed in the Bibliography, and include selected copies of major studies before 1962 and everything we could locate published after that time in Japanese and English.

4. Analysis of voting, demographic, and census data pertaining to Sōka Gakkai–sponsored political candidates from 1955 to 1965.[2]

5. A survey research study, conducted under a grant from the American Council of Learned Societies, of the politico-religious attitudes and behavior of a sample of Tokyo citizens in 1965.

In the following pages, while I shall describe very briefly the history and organization of the Sōka Gakkai, I shall focus on the characteristics of American and Japanese members. Parts of this monograph have appeared elsewhere, though in somewhat modified form. A portion of Chapter I is from my article, "The Sōka Gakkai in Japanese Politics," A *Journal of Church and State*, Spring, 1967. Some of Chapter IV is based on a part of my article "The Sōka Gakkai: A Socio-Political Analysis," *Contemporary Religions in Japan*, September, 1965.

[2] Data on the Sōka Gakkai's political activities are not reported in this monograph. See James Allen Dator, "The Soka Gakkai in Japanese Politics," A *Journal of Church and State*, IX (Spring, 1967), 211–37.

While I am of course indebted to a great many people for aiding me at various points in this research, I would especially like to thank Mr. William P. Woodard, former director of the International Institute for the Study of Religions, Tokyo; Professor Roderick Dugliss, formerly of International Christian University, Tokyo; Professor Jōji Watanuki of the University of Tokyo; Professor Yasumasa Tanaka of Gakushūin University, Tokyo; and Professors Norio Ogata and Jirō Kamishima of Rikkyō University, Tokyo. They are, of course, completely innocent of any errors of fact or interpretation in this report. As far as the division of labor in this study is concerned, while Mr. Niitsu and I worked collaboratively on most phases of the research design and data collection, I alone am responsible for this English edition of our report, and he for a Japanese edition.

JAMES ALLEN DATOR

Virginia Polytechnic Institute

CONTENTS

Preface

I Formation, Organization, Social Beliefs,
and Overseas Expansion   3

II American Members of the Sōka Gakkai   29

III Japanese Members of the Sōka Gakkai   59

IV The Functions and Appeals of the Sōka Gakkai   106

APPENDIXES

I English-Language Tests Given to American Members
of the Sōka Gakkai   143

II Thirty-Item "Traditionalism Scale"
Developed by Tajirō Hayasaka   145

III The Five Personality Scales Used in This Study   147

IV Songs of the Sōka Gakkai   149

Bibliography   151

TABLES

1 Organization of the Sōka Gakkai   6

2 Ethnic Name Distribution of Leaders of the
Sōka Gakkai in North and South America   26

3 Sex, National Origin, and Location
of Overseas Sōka Gakkai Members   27

4 Characteristics of 200 American Members
of the Sōka Gakkai   30

5 New Japanese and American Sōka Gakkai Members
Added Annually   53

6 Characteristics of 200 Japanese Members
of the Sōka Gakkai   60

7 Growth of Sōka Gakkai Household Membership   61

8 Demographic Characteristics of Japanese
Sōka Gakkai Members   68

9 Demographic Characteristics of the
Religious Groups of the 1965 Tokyo Sample   74

10 Six Personality Scales' Percentage
of "Undesirable" Responses   96

11 "Alienation Scale" Responses
of Demographic Categories   103

12 Percentage of Demographic Categories in Each
Religious Group Scoring High on Alienation Scale   104

13 Summary of the Demographic Characteristics
of Religious Groups   122

SŌKA GAKKAI, BUILDERS OF THE THIRD CIVILIZATION

*American
and Japanese Members*

I

FORMATION, ORGANIZATION, SOCIAL BELIEFS, AND OVERSEAS EXPANSION

Formation and Growth

TSUNESABURŌ MAKIGUCHI (1871–1944), a Tokyo elementary school principal and publisher of several books on geography and educational theory, in 1928 entered the Nichiren Shōshū sect of Buddhism.[1] Makiguchi had for some time been working on a series of books on pedagogy, and in 1930 the first of these appeared under the title, *Sōka Kyōiku Taikei* ("A System of Education Based on the Value-creating Principle"). Josei Toda (1900–58) assisted in the preparation of these volumes, and in 1937 these two, along with more than sixty other persons, founded the Sōka Kyōiku Gakkai (Value-creating Education Society) with Makiguchi as president and Toda as chairman. In

---

[1] Nichiren Shōshū ("Shōshū" means, roughly, "True Religion," but the Sōka Gakkai prefers to translate it "True Buddhism") is one of the many sects which are based on the reinterpretation of Buddhism by the Japanese religious leader, Nichiren (1222–82). Adherents of Nichiren Shōshū consider Nichiren to be the true Buddha, replacing the Indian Sakyamuni (563–483 B.C.).

1942 the society began publication of a monthly journal, *Kachi Sōzō* ("Structure of Value"). By this time, Japan was at war, and because the society was opposed to the government's attempt to make Shintō the state religion, the journal was suppressed, and Makiguchi, along with twenty-one other members including Toda, was imprisoned from June, 1943. Membership in the society was said to be about three thousand persons at that time.

Makiguchi died from malnutrition in solitary confinement on November 18, 1944. Toda was released from prison in July, 1945. All but three of the imprisoned members of the Sōka Kyōiku Gakkai had renounced their beliefs and had been released from prison earlier. Indeed, officials of Nichiren Shōshū themselves had instructed the society, which was at that time only loosely affiliated with the Nichiren sect, to comply with the government's requests, but Makiguchi and Toda had steadfastly refused.

The reorganization of the society as a lay organization of the Nichiren Shōshū sect was primarily the work of Josei Toda. In February, 1946, the organization's present name, Sōka Gakkai, was adopted, and in May of the same year the first executive meeting was held. Publication of the monthly study magazine, *Daibyaku Renge* ("White Lotus"), was begun on July 10, 1950, and on April 20, 1951, the newspaper, *Seikyō Shimbun* ("Holy Teaching Newspaper"), was begun.[2]

Toda was chosen president of the society on May 3, 1951, and began a concerted program of conversion, called *shakubuku*, about which we will say more later. In his inaugural speech, Toda pledged attainment of a membership of 750,000 households during his presidency. Since the society had only about 5,000 households at that time, this must have seemed an impossible goal, but by 1958 the membership had passed the mark set by Toda.

[2] The Sōka Gakkai publishes an impressive array of books, journals, and newspapers in English and other languages, in addition to its many Japanese-language publications. Many are cited in the Bibliography. Information about these publications can be gotten by writing the Seikyo Press, 18–29 Shinanomachi, Shinjuku-ku, Tokyo, Japan, or to the Sōka Gakkai Los Angeles Kaikan, 2102 East First Street, Los Angeles, California, 90033.

The period between 1951 and 1958 saw a great many changes in the organization of the Sōka Gakkai, with particular stress being laid upon work among youth. By the time Toda died on April 2, 1958, the Sōka Gakkai was an optimistic, almost geometrically growing group, confident that it was on its way to fulfilling its role of converting the world.

On May 3, 1960, Daisaku Ikeda (1928–   ) was chosen the third and present president of the Sōka Gakkai. Ikeda had been a disciple of Toda since the war, and head of the Youth Division. He was only thirty-two when he became president, an unusually young age for such an office.

The Sōka Gakkai has continued its rapid growth since 1960. It is estimated that the number of households was more than 6,500,000 by July of 1968. It is the largest voluntary organization of any kind in Japan, embracing more than 10 per cent of the total population.[3]

Organizational Features

The Sōka Gakkai has been reorganized several times since its founding. Its structure as of 1966, as shown in Table 1, is one of its most interesting features. The smallest unit, the *kumi*, is kept to a size which permits intense and constant face-to-face

[3] See Table 7 showing the growth of the Sōka Gakkai. Determining the actual membership of the Sōka Gakkai is very difficult, since as with most Japanese religions, membership is determined by counting not individuals, but households (*setai*). Membership, thus, is reckoned on the basis of the number of Gohonzon distributed (the Gohonzon is explained below). A Gohonzon mandala is given to the first person of each household who is converted to Nichiren Shōshū. The membership count is then cumulative. Apparently no subtraction is made from the total for members who lapse in faith. The total number of individual members in the Sōka Gakkai is typically determined by multiplying the total household membership by two, two and a half, or three. Obviously the results vary greatly.

That the Sōka Gakkai's official estimate of its household membership is probably in error is indicated, but not proven, by the fact that the ratio of Sōka Gakkai vote in each election to the official household membership at that time has steadily declined. According to the *Asahi Shimbun*, July 13, 1965, in the 1955 House of Councillors election, the ratio was 2.44 votes per household; in 1959, 2.32; in 1962, 1.52; and in 1965 it was 0.56 votes per household. See also Baiyu Watanabe, "Sūji Kara Mita Shin-Shūkyō," *Daihōrin*, March, 1964, pp. 100–6.

TABLE 1
Organization of the Sōka Gakkai*

Top hierarchy:
- President
- General Directors / Vice General Directors / Directors
- General Administration
- Central Headquarters (chūō hombu)

Affiliated organizations (across top):
- Asian Peoples' Association — Institute of Oriental Science
- Democratic Music & Drama Associations (Min'on & Min'en)

Divisions under Central Headquarters:
- Pilgrimage Division
- Culture Division
  - Public Opinion Department
  - Art Department
  - Education Department
  - Science Department
  - Economics Department
- Financial Division
- Study Division
- Overseas Bureau
  - Headquarters
  - General Headquarters
  - Chapters

Publications:
- Ushio Publications
- Seikyo Press

Clean Government Party (Kōmeitō) (formally separate)

Local Headquarters (chihō hombu):
- General block
- Subgeneral block
- Major block
- Block
- Minor block

Men's Division:
- General Chapter (sōshibu)
- Chapter (shibu)
- District (chiku)
- Group (han)
- Unit (buntai)

Women's Division:
- General Chapter (sōshibu)
- Chapter (shibu)
- District (chiku)
- Group (han)
- Unit (kumi)

Youth Division:

	Boys' & Girls' Division	Junior High Division	High School Division	College Students' Division	Young Women's Division	Young Men's Division
	Subdivision (bu)	Subdivision (bu)	Subdivision (bu)	Subdivision (bu)	Subdivision (bu)	Subdivision (bu)
					Corps (butai)	Corps (butai)
					Ward (ku)	Company (tai)
	Group (han)	Group (han)	Group (han)	Group (han)	Group (han)	Group (han)
	Unit (kumi)	Unit (kumi)	Unit (kumi)	Unit (kumi)	Unit (kumi)	Unit (buntai)

contacts, especially in the *zadankai* (discussion meetings) between a small number of members. When a *kumi* becomes too
large, it simply divides amoeba-like into two *kumi*, continuing
the process as members enter the organization. Thus the individual need not feel the alienating effects of bigness which is
so much a feature of mass organization.

Moreover, the structure of the Sōka Gakkai seems well designed to fix the individual in a web of interlocking small-group
activities. This structural relationship can be conceptualized as
having three dimensions. There is first the relationship based
on conversion ties, viewed as a vertical organization. This
stretches from the individual (considered theoretically and as-
pirationally as a household); to the *kumi* (unit, 10 to 15 members); to the *han* (group, 30 to 100 members); to the *chiku*
(district, 500 to 1,000 members; there are about 15,500 districts
in Japan and 475 overseas); the *shibu* (chapter, of which there
are about 1,825 in Japan and 54 overseas); the *chihō hombu*
(local headquarters, 109 in Japan and 6 overseas); and the
chūō hombu (central headquarters, located in Tokyo).

Since this "vertical" relation is based on conversion ties (a
person is a member of the *kumi* of the person who converted
him even after he gets his own *kumi* of persons whom he converted; *han* then are composed of members converted by the
same group of people, and so forth), in Japan's highly mobile
society, it soon became evident that a Sōka Gakkai member
who moved from one area to another could be living next
door to another Sōka Gakkai member and never know it. Thus,
a "horizontal," geographically based structure was developed,
called the "block system." This includes a series of geographical
units, in size about the same as the vertical structure, which
permits Sōka Gakkai members who live in the same area to
be in close contact with each other.[4]

Finally, there is a system of interest or peer-group organizations, which can be conceptualized as a "diagonal" structure,
which is intended to fix the individual even more strongly in

[4] As will be seen below, *kumi* and block meetings are most frequently
held in members' homes, while the larger groups meet in rented public,
or Sōka Gakkai–owned, halls. Nichiren Shōshū temples are used primarily
only for the "baptism" services (*gojukai*), for private or group prayer,
or for special "holy day" services.

the organization by satisfying his needs for interaction with persons of his own age, sex, and/or interests. Thus there is a Youth Division which includes divisions for young men (1966 membership: 1,800,000), young women (1,500,000), and a division each for students in college (100,000), high school, junior high school, and the elementary grades. There are a division for women, and one for men; the Study Department (1,175,000);[5] athletic groups; a culture organization for music and dance, called Min'on (Democratic Music Association, 780,000); one for drama, called Min'en (Democratic Drama Association); and a political party, called the Kōmeitō, which polled 5,097,173 votes, or 13.5 per cent of the votes cast, in the July 4, 1965, House of Councillors election and which is generally considered to be the "third power" in Japan.[6] The Sōka Gakkai plans to complete by 1972 an educational complex from elementary school through college (the university to be called Sōka Daigaku). Consideration has also been given to establishing a labor union, and perhaps other economically oriented groups (members are encouraged to do business with other Sōka Gakkai members even now).

In a culture, such as the Japanese, which emphasizes small-group cooperation and yet where there are said to be many alienated individuals, the Sōka Gakkai seems to be well organized to exploit these societal deficiencies and provide the individual with the physical and psychological certainties he seeks, and yet, because of its cellular structure, grow to be a mass organization.

[5] See Appendix I for examples of examinations given by the Study Department for promotion to the various teaching ranks within the Sōka Gakkai.

[6] For a description of the growth of the Kōmeitō, see James Allen Dator, "The Sōka Gakkai in Japanese Politics," A Journal of Church and State, IX (Spring, 1967), 211–37.

Political and Social Beliefs [7]

There is a question of whether the Sōka Gakkai was really philosophically dependent on the Nichiren Shōshū sect during the time Tsunesaburō Makiguchi was president. Makiguchi himself seems to have been more concerned with his Kachiron (philosophy of value), which was developed almost independently of influence from Nichiren Buddhistic thought and is largely pragmatic and Kantian. It is said, indeed, that even those parts of Kachiron that clearly come from Nichiren were added later, probably by Josei Toda, after Makiguchi's death.[8]

Be that as it may, ever since Toda's presidency the Sōka Gakkai has quite consciously based its beliefs on Nichiren's thought, as interpreted by the Nichiren Shōshū. Thus, in order to appreciate the philosophical basis of the Sōka Gakkai's political and social activities, it is necessary to understand something of the interpretation of Nichiren that the Sōka Gakkai adopts.

At the base of the Sōka Gakkai's beliefs are the three "secrets" (Sandai Hihō) of Nichiren: "Honmon no Honzon," "Honmon no Daimoku," and "Honmon no Kaidan."

Simply put, Honmon no Honzon is the exclusive object of worship, the Gohonzon, which is the mandala upon which Nichiren himself is said to have written the essence of the Buddhist Law. The original mandala, the Dai-Gohonzon, is kept at the sect's main temple, Taiseki-ji, near Mt. Fuji.[9] But each believer, after he performs the service (called Gojukai) that makes him a formal member of Nichiren Shōshū, receives a replica Gohonzon which he places in his home and before which he says his daily prayers.[10] The Gohonzon is considered

---

[7] This account of the Sōka Gakkai's social and political philosophy is derived solely from Sōka Gakkai sources. If the statements made in the following pages seem vague to the reader, it must be pointed out that we have attempted only to paraphrase what the Sōka Gakkai has itself published. See the Bibliography for sources.

[8] Noel Brannen, "The Soka Gakkai's Theory of Value," *Contemporary Religions in Japan*, V (June, 1964), 151–4.

[9] Many scholars doubt that this is actually the mandala which Nichiren wrote himself.

[10] As we pointed out above, actually, each household receives a Gohonzon, not each individual member.

to be Nichiren, to embody Nichiren, not merely to represent him or his thought. There is, in effect, a doctrine of "real presence" in the Gohonzon. Moreover, since Nichiren himself is believed to be the True Buddha, the Gohonzon has enormous importance and power as an object of worship.

The second secret, Honmon no Daimoku, are the words, Nam-myōhō-renge-kyō ("All hail to the Lotus Sutra"), which the believer chants over and over as a prayer. The believer receives enlightenment, divine benefit, protection, the granting of a request, or whatever he desires through the repetition of these sacred words of praise to the Lotus Sutra. Honmon no Kaidan, the third secret, is the sacred altar that will be built after the completion of kōsenrufu (world-wide propagation of the [Nichiren] faith). The Kaidan will house the Dai Gohonzon and will be the source of all power and faith on earth.

The essence of these three secrets is expressed in the phrase, Shiki shin funi, which means that matter (shiki) and spirit (shin) are not two things (funi), but one. Nichiren Shōshū stresses the unity of mind and matter, and criticizes other religions and philosophies—for example, Christianity on the one hand and Marxism on the other—which try to establish a world view based on the supremacy of either mind over matter or matter over mind. This unity of mind and matter is the basis of the Sōka Gakkai's teaching concerning the individual, his problems, and their cure, and it is also the source of the Sōka Gakkai's social beliefs in general and its political beliefs in particular.

The phrase used to summarize this philosophy is Ōbutsu myōgō which means the unity (myōgō) of secular law (ō-hō, ō meaning "king") and sacred law (buppō, the law of Buddha). Thus, the Sōka Gakkai maintains that the governance of society must be based on the complete integration of the law of the state with the law of the universe, as revealed by Nichiren.[11]

At the present time, says the Sōka Gakkai, no nation bases its

[11] Nichiren explains this relation in his Risshō Ankoku Ron, which are writings concerned with the problem of correct government. The Sōka Gakkai considers its political philosophy to be a modern adaptation of Risshō Ankoku Ron.

laws on the True Law of the universe. Hence, society is in turmoil, and each individual's life is one of sickness, privation, and misery. Thus, while the individual can achieve substantial and immediate benefit through conversion to Nichiren Shōshū, he cannot achieve total happiness until society is converted as well, and until the rulers of society are adherents of Nichiren Shōshū.

Japan is guaranteed through its Constitution a democratic government, which means, the Sōka Gakkai simply states, a government of, by, and for the people. But as a matter of fact, it claims, the government of Japan is one of corrupt politicians, by corrupt politicians, and for corrupt politicians.[12] The wishes of the people are ignored. This is an intolerable situation, and yet it can be easily remedied by placing Sōka Gakkai members in positions of power. In a modern democratic nation, this of course can only be done through the electoral process. Thus, obviously, the Sōka Gakkai must nominate and elect members of Nichiren Shōshū to government.

There is nothing in this, insists the Sōka Gakkai, which violates the constitutional provision of the separation of religion and politics.[13] The Sōka Gakkai maintains that it does not seek to make Nichiren Shōshū the state religion. Rather, as is the case of any other group that thinks it has a complete political theory based upon the people's genuine desires, it

[12] "Japanese religion is in the 16th Century, its politics is in the 18th Century, and its economics is in the 19th Century. . . . Only its Constitution is 20th Century." From a round-table discussion by Sōka Gakkai leaders concerning Japanese politics, *Daibyaku Renge*, July, 1964, pp. 28–29.

[13] Article 20 of the Japanese Constitution states:

"Freedom of religion is guaranteed to all. No religious organization shall receive any privileges from the State, nor exercise any political authority.

"No person shall be compelled to take part in any religious act, celebration, rite or practice.

"The State and its organs shall refrain from religious education or any religious activity."

Article 89 adds: "No public money or other property shall be expended or appropriated for the use, benefit or maintenance of any religious institutions, or for any charitable, educational or benevolent enterprises not under the control of public authority."

seeks to place in government persons who understand and will work for the satisfaction of the people's true will.[14]

Democracy, says the Sōka Gakkai, is based upon liberty, equality, and dignity.[15] Both major forms of democracy today— European (liberal) democracy and Marxist (people's) democracy—have great contradictions in them because they are not based upon *shiki shin funi* (the unity of mind and matter). European democracy, which finds its source in Christianity, overemphasizes the spiritual at the expense of the material, the Sōka Gakkai claims. Thus Western democracy exalts the spiritual value of "freedom" with the result that great masses of men are thrown into poverty by the "free" economy; others, such as Negroes in America, are persecuted by the "free" society; and many more persons, alienated and anomic by modern urbanized and mechanized life, yearn to escape from freedom by adopting various totalitarian and false religions and philosophies.

Marxist democracy, on the other hand, though attempting to solve the problems caused by liberal democracy, stresses only the material side of life, the Sōka Gakkai maintains. The result is a social system that enslaves the people. Moreover, Marxist democracy is ambivalent concerning the meaning of "equality." While apparently willing to drag all men down to the same level, and unwilling to permit superior humans to excel, it assumes that the problems of the world are caused by the organization of society by and for a certain class, and that if that class—the capitalist—is removed and a dictatorship of the proletariat is imposed, a utopian society will result.

[14] The Sōka Gakkai repeatedly, although not very convincingly, tries to distinguish *ōbutsu myōgō* from two historical types of union of religion and politics. One, *saisei itchi*, is the ancient relation between religion and government in Japan where *sai* (the performance of religious ceremonies) and *sei* (government) were combined (*itchi*). That is, in ancient times the primary function of the government was to see that religious services were performed properly and on time.

Seikyō itchi is used to describe church and state relations as were found, for example, in medieval Christendom. *Sei*, again, is "government," and *kyō* is "religion." For a fuller explanation of both of these concepts, see *Daibyaku Renge*, December, 1962, pp. 16–17.

[15] *Songen* (dignity, majesty, or augustness) is the term used to express the idea of the supreme value of the life of each individual. The Sōka Gakkai avoids the more common third term, "fraternity."

Finally, both liberal and Marxist democracy, the Sōka Gakkai claims, treat human beings as things, and not as individuals. They do not understand the dignity of each individual, and the preciousness of each individual's life.

Buddhist democracy, based upon Buddhist law which understands the unity of spirit and matter, will, insists the Sōka Gakkai, establish a society where each individual is truly free, equal and respected.

A great problem of the present time, the Sōka Gakkai teaches, is the apathy of the people induced by the alienating dislocations of liberal and Marxist democracy. The people want peace, but present governments are headed toward war. The people want prosperity, but there is unemployment, poverty, and hardship everywhere. The people want health, but more and more people die of cancer and other modern diseases every day. The people want happiness now, but their lives are full of misery.

Yet everything the people want, the Sōka Gakkai insists, is immediately within their reach through True Buddhism. Thus the people must be roused from their apathy to achieve the things they desire. True democracy must be based on the sovereignty of each individual, and the active participation in politics of all people and all classes. The purpose of the Kōmeitō, the political arm of the Sōka Gakkai, is to help individuals achieve the happiness they seek.[16] The main political slogan of the Sōka Gakkai is "for the realization of a society which combines the happiness of the individual with the prosperity of all [society]," [17] thus emphasizing both individual and collective needs.

Ōbutsu myōgō, the unity of sacred and secular law, as mentioned above, can be described as having four particular

[16] "Politics is like the management of a household. If the family as a whole participates in making decisions, it is a harmonious and happy democracy. But if the husband makes all the decisions it is dictatorial, one-man rule. The principle of government for the state is the same. All members must participate." *Daibyaku Renge*, August, 1964, p. 19.

[17] In Japanese, this is *Kojin no kōfuku to shakai no han-ei ga itchi suru shakai no jitsugen*. The Sōka Gakkai uses it frequently now. See, for one example, *Daibyaku Renge*, July, 1964, p. 19. In an earlier form, the word order was reversed with the "prosperity of society" coming before the "happiness of the individual." See *Daibyaku Renge*, June, 1962, p. 18.

manifestations. The first is the cultural aspect which combines, through True Buddhism, the best of Western Christian (spiritual) culture with the best of Marxist (material) culture to produce what the Sōka Gakkai calls the "Third Civilization" (Daisan Bunmei). By infusing the educational system with True Buddhism, by basing the arts on Nichiren's teachings, by coupling the scientific theology of Nichiren with modern science and medicine, and by helping the masses lead their lives creatively and purposefully, the Sōka Gakkai promises that the highest civilization possible to man will result.

The second aspect of *ōbutsu myōgō* is economic. Here also, the best of capitalist society—that which encourages individual initiative and gives each individual the freedom to choose an occupation best suited to his abilities and interests—will be adopted. But at the same time, respect for labor and agriculture, and the recognition that society is obligated to see that the basic physical and spiritual needs of *all* men be guaranteed through an extensive social welfare program, will be adopted from socialism. This economic attitude the Sōka Gakkai calls "neosocialism" (*shin shakaishugi*).

Third, in order to secure world peace, the Sōka Gakkai promises to establish a society which accepts and utilizes the unique character of each nation and race, but which also recognizes the necessity of world unity through the establishment of a world-wide community. This it calls "world brotherhood" (*chikyū minzokushugi*; literally, "world racialism").

Finally, by combining the best of Western democracy and Marxist democracy with the teachings of Nichiren as outlined above, the Sōka Gakkai intends to establish a political system guaranteeing freedom, equality, and dignity to all individuals. This the Sōka Gakkai entitles "Buddhist democracy" (*buppō minshushugi*).

The preceding description of the Sōka Gakkai's founding, structure, and beliefs has been purposely quite brief, so that while the reader will have some general understanding of the society, he will not be led to prejudge it until he has, as it were, seen it from the inside. In the later chapters, we will turn to the Sōka Gakkai's own media and to available survey data, in an attempt to see what the Sōka Gakkai members, both American and Japanese, are like, and what they expect from the Sōka Gakkai. But before doing that, we will consider briefly the expansion of the Sōka Gakkai overseas.

Overseas Expansion

The data in this brief report of the development of the overseas branches of the Sōka Gakkai come primarily from the Sōka Gakkai's own media, the *Seikyō Shimbun, Seikyō Graphic,* and *Daisan Bunmei.* We also interviewed members of the Sōka Gakkai's Overseas Bureau, and surveyed non–Sōka Gakkai media.

The Sōka Gakkai did not become formally involved in overseas work until after Daisaku Ikeda became president in 1960. Of course, former president Josei Toda was interested in overseas activities of the Sōka Gakkai, and the *Seikyō Shimbun* did occasionally print articles about the experiences of individual Sōka Gakkai members overseas. But there was no formal mechanism within the organization for handling problems of overseas expansion, nor does it seem that these problems were taken care of by any other department in a systematic way. There are two simple reasons for this: the number of Japanese Sōka Gakkai members that went overseas in the early period was very small, and there were practically no foreign members within the Sōka Gakkai either in Japan or overseas.

Because traditionally a person's religious affiliation in Japan is determined by that of his family and/or the area in which he lives, there has been no tradition in Japan for aggressive proselytizing activities by religious groups such as seems to be considered normal for Christianity. Developing leaders in the Sōka Gakkai who would and could convert others took time and skill. Until problems of internal purpose and unity were solved, consideration of external expansion, especially overseas, had to wait.

In addition, the attitude of the Sōka Gakkai toward foreigners was and remains ambivalent. Nichiren was a Japanese, and there has been a strong sense of the superiority and "holiness" of Japan in contrast to "heathen" nations. At the same time Japanese members of the Sōka Gakkai, in common with most other Japanese, evidence a distinct sense of inferiority toward Westerners.[18]

As we saw, the Sōka Gakkai is especially concerned with establishing its position against what it considers to be the two major intellectual streams of Western culture; the "spiritual," as found in Christianity, and the "material," as evidenced by Marxism. But there is something of the old Greater East Asian Co-Prosperity Sphere in its attitude toward other Asian peoples. For example, an article in the *Seikyō Shimbun* in 1960, entitled "The Superiority of the Japanese Race," had this to say:

The basic problem is whether or not they have the ability to understand Mahayana Buddhism. Throughout all the world, the only people who are able to understand the essence of Mahayana Buddhism—specifically, the meaning of *Nam-myōhō-renge-kyō*—are Japanese. Only the Japanese can understand the True Philosophy of [Nichiren] Daishōnin. Therefore, we who can understand must teach those who cannot understand.[19]

1. *Development of the overseas organization.* It seems that the existence of Sōka Gakkai members overseas came about not by the conversion of non-Japanese overseas, nor even by the return home of foreigners converted in Japan, but by Japanese Sōka Gakkai members moving abroad. The earliest figures we could find (June, 1960) indicated that there were 710 Sōka Gakkai members overseas: 466 in North America, 113 in South America, 45 in the Republic of China, 36 in the Republic of Korea, 16 in Indonesia, 7 in the Philippines, 10 in Red China, 4 in North Korea, 4 in Australia, 2 in India, and 1 each in

[18] For data on Japanese attitudes toward foreigners, see Jōichi Suetsuna et al., *Nihonjin no Kokuminsei* (Tōkyō: Shiseidō, 1961), English résumé, p. 27; Tooru Yoshimura, "Nihonjin no Aikokushin," *Jiyū*, March, 1965, p. 28; C. Martin Wilbur, "Some Findings of Japanese Opinion Polls," pp. 300–15, in Hugh Borton (ed.), *Japan Between East and West* (New York: Harper and Row, 1957); Michiya Shimbari et al., "Measuring a Nation's Prestige," *American Journal Of Sociology*, LXIX (July, 1963), 63–68.

[19] *Seikyō Shimbun*, October 8, 1960.

Burma, Jordan, Singapore, Italy, West Germany, France, and Egypt.[20]

In the same issue of the *Seikyō Shimbun* that contained these figures, General Secretary Hojo observed that "since May, the strength of the Sōka Gakkai overseas has increased. Everyday, the Central Headquarters [in Tokyo] gets more and more letters from members who have gone abroad, and daily it seems that about two or three more members go to such places as India and America."

Among the items in these letters to the Central Headquarters were requests for publications in English and other foreign languages that would help the members in their attempts to convert others by explaining the teachings of the Sōka Gakkai. These overseas members, though affiliated with some chapter or district in Japan, were going about their work on an entirely individual basis. There was no machinery for systematic communication with and among overseas members.

One of the first changes that occurred after Daisaku Ikeda became president in May, 1960, was the establishment of a formal organization to help guide the overseas members and put persons living in the same area in touch with each other. Specifically, on July 15, 1960, an Overseas Branch (Kaigai Kei) was set up at first within the General Affairs Division (Shōmu Bu), and then as a separate bureau within the Central Headquarters. The activities of the Overseas Branch were essentially threefold: (1) to provide appropriate translated material; (2) to advise and guide members living overseas; and (3) to guide foreign members living in Japan. Also, until this time, a person converted overseas would receive his Gohonzon from the chapter of the person who converted him, after first receiving the permission of the chapter. After the establishment of the Overseas Branch, new members received their Gohonzon directly from that organization.

In October of 1960, the same year the Overseas Branch

[20] *Seikyō Shimbun*, July 15, 1960. At the same time, there were 5,886 members in Okinawa. While Okinawa is not yet under the jurisdiction of Japan, it was listed by the *Seikyō Shimbun* with the Japanese totals, and not as overseas.

was set up, President Ikeda made a trip to North and South America to view the work of the Sōka Gakkai there. During that time, he established two chapters, one in Los Angeles for North America, and another in Brazil for South America. Together they formed the American General Chapter, which had an initial staff of thirty-eight persons.

On January 28, 1961, President Ikeda visited India, Burma, Thailand, and Cambodia in order to view firsthand the condition of Buddhism in these countries and especially to see the birthplace of the founder of Buddhism, Sakyamuni. Ikeda stated that this was to be the start of the conversion of Southeast Asia to True Buddhism, and to serve as the basis for world-wide conversion. For this purpose, a Southeast Asia Chapter was established, and a unified attempt at *shakubuku*, under the direction of the Central Headquarters, was begun. Since that time, representatives from the Central Headquarters have made a number of overseas visits yearly to various countries, including the Soviet Union.[21]

To help satisfy the need for English language material, on October 2, 1961, the English-language volume, *The Sokagakkai*, was published, and on May 15, 1962, the publication of the *Seikyo News* began on a bimonthly basis. Since then, as the

[21] Below is a record of overseas trips taken by President Ikeda or other high officials of the Sōka Gakkai from 1960 to 1965, as compiled from reports in the *Seikyō Shimbun*.

1960	October	America, Canada, Brazil
1961	January	India, Ceylon, Burma, Thailand, Hong Kong
	May	Taiwan, Philippines, Thailand, Hong Kong
	August	America, Brazil, Paraguay
	October	Denmark, West Germany, Holland, France, England, Spain, Switzerland, Austria, Italy
1962	January	Iran, Iraq, Turkey, Greece, Egypt, Pakistan
	August	Taiwan, Philippines, Vietnam, Thailand, Burma, Hong Kong
1963	January	Around the world trip, covering eleven countries, and all areas having Sōka Gakkai groups in North and South America
	October	Soviet Union and Europe
1964	May	Australia, Indonesia, India
	August	South America, Los Angeles
	October	Middle East and European countries
1965	August	United States

bibliography shows, there has been an increasing number of publications, not only in English but in other foreign languages as well. Unfortunately the literary quality and grammatical accuracy of the English-language publications are quite low even though the layout and photography are generally satisfactory to excellent.

At the same time, the Japanese-language media began devoting increasing amounts of space to the activities of overseas members. For example, in 1956 the *Seikyō Shimbun* carried only four articles about overseas activities, in 1957 ten, and in 1958 eleven. In 1960 the figure jumped to 87, and in 1961 to 148. Since then, there have been several hundred articles yearly about overseas members. Similar increases in space and prominence are found in the Japanese-language *Seikyō Graphic*, with a portion of each issue since 1966 devoted to describing and depicting in some detail foreign areas, even those which may not have Sōka Gakkai members, in what appears to be a concentrated effort to raise the Japanese members' level of interest in foreign matters. This series is titled "Let's Go to the World!" (*Sekai ni Ikoo*). There are in addition other articles, proclaiming such sentiments as "Youth, to the world!" (*Seinen yo Sekai e*), which, amid beautiful travelogue pictures, describe the climate, products, culture, and people of various areas, and the obligation of the Sōka Gakkai to bring True Buddhism to them.

Thus, the interest of the Sōka Gakkai in overseas missions has increased tremendously, and attempts to convert foreigners living in Japan—an activity within the realm of possibility for the average Sōka Gakkai member, whereas a trip abroad is not—have been greatly applauded. The persons most vulnerable to Sōka Gakkai presentation are American military personnel, particularly those who frequent the bars around the bases.

Contacts between Japanese and foreigners generally are found only at three levels—between the Japanese business community and their foreign counterparts; between Japanese students and foreigners willing to instruct them in a foreign language; and between Japanese shop and bar clerks and their foreign customers and Japanese maids and their foreign employers. Because, as we will see, there appear to be very few Japanese Sōka Gakkai members among the upper and upper-middle strata, foreigners in the business and cultural community seldom meet a member of the Sōka Gakkai. Contact at the second level also seems rare, but the chances of a foreigner meeting a Sōka Gakkai shop clerk or bar hostess are very good. However, it is only in the latter instance that an opportunity for serious communication is likely to occur.

For a time the Sōka Gakkai attempted to capitalize on this fact. An article in the *Seikyō Graphic* in 1962, "The 'Base' for Overseas Conversion," told about activities around Tachikawa Air Force Base, near Tokyo:

These splendid people are bar and cabaret hostesses who work at night in Tachikawa. These women, in the process of deepening their own faith, are converting many American soldiers to True Buddhism. Generally, the contact between these men and women is only temporary, but many Sōka Gakkai women have succeeded in marrying an American. Observing the deep faith which these women have, many of the men are giving up their Christian beliefs and joining the Sōka Gakkai. In this way, Sōka Gakkai members will be returning to each part of America, to further the conversion of the American continent.[22]

Recently, however, the Sōka Gakkai has played down this type of activity, apparently because of criticisms from Western journalists, such as those found in *Time, Newsweek,* and *Look.* Articles about conversions of soldiers are now rare in the Sōka Gakkai media, and in their place are the travelogue features mentioned above.

The result of all these various aspects of the Sōka Gakkai's overseas spread is an overseas organization composed of five local headquarters, eight general chapters, fifty-four chapters, and a roughly estimated household membership of 50,000 in North America, 25,000 in South America, 15,000 in Southeast Asia, 1,500 in Europe (mostly in Germany and France), and 75,000 in Okinawa. In the United States there are Sōka Gakkai groups in Honolulu, Oahu, Seattle, San Francisco, Oakland, Long Beach, Hollywood, Los Angeles, San Diego, St.

---

[22] *Seikyō Graphic,* March 22, 1962, p. 14.

Louis, Chicago, New York, Washington, D.C., Kentucky, Carolina, Texas, Colorado, Kansas, and Michigan.

We have described very briefly the development of Sōka Gakkai organizations overseas and the establishment of bodies within the Sōka Gakkai in Japan to handle overseas affairs. Now we wish to turn to a problem that will interest us in the following chapters. Namely, what kinds of people are the overseas members, and what sorts of activities are they carrying out?

In the next chapter we will use the English-language *Seikyo News* to gain some understanding of the Sōka Gakkai's American members. Now we will use Japanese-language sources, primarily the *Seikyō Shimbun* and the *Seikyō Graphic,* to learn about the characteristics of Japanese Sōka Gakkai members who are overseas. From these sources, we can make four general classifications of overseas Japanese members: (1) Japanese women married to Americans, usually to military personnel but occasionally to civilians, who are now residents in the United States or in American military bases in Europe and elsewhere; (2) Japanese emigrants to South America, predominantly to Brazil, Peru, Bolivia, or Argentina, and to a far lesser extent to North America; (3) representatives of Japanese business firms in North and South America, Southeast Asia, Australia, and Europe; (4) Japanese students in the United States and Europe.

There is relatively little mention in Sōka Gakkai media of the latter two categories, and as other evidence will also indicate, apparently their number is very small. Thus, we shall concentrate on the first two groups of overseas Sōka Gakkai members.

2. *Japanese members in the United States.* The Sōka Gakkai's overseas expansion began first in the United States, to some extent because for political, economic, and military reasons, Japanese communication with the United States is greater than with any other country at the present time, but specifically because many Japanese Sōka Gakkai members in the United States seem to be the wives of American military personnel.

As we will see, in Japan, few of the Sōka Gakkai members

have a high level of education or a high standard of living. Most live in factory and small shop districts and many may dream of going to the United States or elsewhere in order to gain a better life. But the people who seem best able to achieve this are the women, apparently mainly bar and cabaret hostesses, who marry American G.I.'s. We found, for example, that of the 38 staff members of the American General Chapter that was established in November, 1960, 26 of them (68 per cent) were Japanese women. This is a far greater proportion of women than are found among general chapter leaders in Japan. In addition, of the 29 Sōka Gakkai members in America whose activities and experiences were reported in the *Seikyō Shimbun* in the year following the establishment of the American General Chapter, 23 were women.

Miss Yasu Kashiwabara, a prominent Sōka Gakkai female member, reported the following about her encounter with Japanese female Sōka Gakkai members in the United States:

Since the organization of the Sōka Gakkai in the United States dates only from 1960, it is, of course, not very old. At that time, I accompanied President Ikeda on his trip to the United States and met many of the war brides (*senso hanayome*) who were Sōka Gakkai members there. I had heard that these women were leading lonely and isolated lives, and one purpose of my trip was to see what could be done for them.

There to greet us at the Los Angeles Airport were about twenty or thirty war brides, many of them accompanied by their husbands. Because their husbands were GI's, their lives were not very good. There was no one who owned a car, and it was necessary to rent one just to get President Ikeda to his hotel. Thus I could see that their standard of living was not very high. Of course, as war brides, their lives were miserable and they were isolated from society. I felt that they needed even greater faith than they had had in Japan. And yet, these war brides had been separated even from each other. When they saw one another at the airport, they said in surprise, "Are you here too?" The situation was of course intolerable, and it was necessary to organize at once. Thus, the purpose of the organization was not to engage in missionary work, but rather it arose naturally in response to this situation.[23]

[23] From the popular women's magazine, *Shūkan Myōjō*, December 20, 1964, p. 104.

It seems, then, that the overseas organization of the Sōka Gakkai was designed primarily to comfort and strengthen in faith Japanese female members in the United States. These women probably ranged from fervent believers to those with only the slightest interest in the Sōka Gakkai, but Miss Kashiwabara and others apparently recognized that the prerequisite to successful propagation abroad was the unification of this Japanese "remnant." Thus, for some time, work was conducted almost exclusively by and for these women. Discussion meetings (*zadankai*) were conducted in Japanese, and many participants were Japanese women. In addition, as the following quotation shows, *shakubuku* was mainly performed by the Japanese members on other Japanese living nearby.

For the first two or three years, *shakubuku* and other Sōka Gakkai activities were performed mainly by the Japanese. We would look up Japanese-sounding names in the telephone book, take a bus out to the area, find the house, and begin *shakubuku*. I remember those days very well.[24]

The situation, however, seems to be changing. For example, recently, President Ikeda, in addition to exhorting the members to deepen their faith, has advised them to master English, get a driver's permit, and become American citizens.[25] The *Seikyō Shimbun* reported the following concerning the Washington, D.C., Chapter in 1966:

Group meetings are held once a week. District and Chapter meetings are also held. In spite of the fact that many of the women here have trouble with English, all of these meetings are held in English. Nowadays, only the lectures on the Gosho [the sacred writings of Nichiren] are in Japanese.[26]

Miss Kashiwabara also has this to say in the article cited above:

We still are not making any special efforts towards conversion. There is of course no essential difference between the way Americans and Japanese are converted. By showing actual proof, people

[24] Report by a Japanese wife of the activities of the San Francisco Chapter, in the *Seikyō Graphic*, April 26, 1966.
[25] *Daibyaku Renge*, May, 1966.
[26] *Seikyō Shimbun*, April 10, 1966.

will join. However, rather than having Japanese convert Americans, we must have Americans converting Americans. Until that stage is reached, the progress of the Sōka Gakkai in the United States cannot be very rapid. . . . As the number of foreigners increases, group discussion meetings too must be conducted in English, and English must be used for technical Buddhist words. For example, rather than talking about *shakubuku*, an English equivalent must be found. Next spring, the first Study Department Examinations will be held by the American headquarters, and we need to begin thinking about how the overseas structure of the Sōka Gakkai, which was originally established to aid the overseas Japanese, should be altered for the benefit of the American members.[27]

The influence of the American husbands of these Japanese members may be beginning to permeate slowly. When we interviewed the chief of the Overseas Bureau at the Tokyo Headquarters, he said that the planting of Nichiren Shōshū in the United States "was clearly connected with these marriages, but it will have to be through the husbands of these Japanese women that the faith will spread. Still, these Japanese women have made a very important contribution." [28]

When we review the preceding, we come to the conclusion that Sōka Gakkai activities in the United States were begun mainly by Japanese female members and to a lesser extent by their American husbands and by Japanese males in the United States. The number and influence of non-Japanese women especially seems to have been extremely slight. Nisei and Sansei Japanese-American citizens have appeared frequently among the leaders, and only a few non-Japanese Americans who appear to have no marital or other connections with Japan have also joined.

3. *Sōka Gakkai members in South America.* The spread of the Sōka Gakkai to South America, unlike the United States, was principally due to Japanese emigrants. These Sōka Gakkai emigrants were primarily males or married couples engaged in agricultural occupations.[29]

The formal organization of the Sōka Gakkai came about during President Ikeda's trip of October, 1960, that we have

[27] *Shūkan Myōjō.*
[28] Interview with Chief Morita of the Overseas Office, June 6, 1966.
[29] *Seikyō Shimbun,* October 29, 1960.

mentioned before. But the spread of the Sōka Gakkai in South America was far slower than in the United States partly because of the fact that the members generally lived in widely scattered rural areas, and were handicapped by inadequate transportation and communication facilities. Thus it was difficult for members to meet one another. However, by mid-1966, there were twelve chapters in South America, located in Brazil (the largest number of members are there and this is the site of the South American Headquarters), Peru, Bolivia, Argentina, Paraguay, and the Dominican Republic.

Some Nisei and Sansei have been converted, and the number of members of non-Japanese lineage may be increasing as well,[30] but the Sōka Gakkai in South America, as in North America, seems predominantly to continue to appeal to, and to be controlled by, Japanese or persons of Japanese national origin.

Our classification of the names given in the *Seikyo Times* as the leaders in the North and South American chapters is shown in Table 2. From these data we conclude that (1) persons of Japanese origin control both the North and South American Sōka Gakkai chapters; (2) the South American leaders appear to be entirely of Japanese national origin; (3) in both North and South America the leadership is about evenly split between women and men, but in North America, 28 per cent of the leaders are apparently the Japanese wives of American men, another 18 per cent are women with entirely Japanese names, and only 22 per cent of the leaders are males having entirely American names; (4) in addition, in North America male leaders of Japanese national origin outnumber those of native American origin; (5) the size of the North American organization is larger than that of the South American group; (6) although this is not shown in the table, apparently sixteen of the American leaders (19 per cent) were husband and wife. In four pairs, both husband and wife had

---

[30] "What has been the pattern of Shakubuku recently?"

"Now there are more foreigners than Japanese becoming members. Recently, of the thirty persons interviewed to become *taichō*, only two were Japanese and the rest were Nisei or Brazilians. In all of the chapters now, about 2/5 of the members are Japanese, 2/5 are Nisei, and 1/5 are Brazilians." From the *Seikyō Shimbun*, July 30, 1966.

TABLE 2

ETHNIC NAME DISTRIBUTION OF LEADERS OF THE SŌKA GAKKAI
IN NORTH AND SOUTH AMERICA
(In Per Cent)

NORTH AMERICA		SOUTH AMERICA	
Male		Male	
Japanese or Nisei	24	Japanese or Nisei	50
Nisei	6	Nisei	0
Non-Japanese	22	Non-Japanese	0
Female		Female	
Japanese and Western	28	Japanese and Western	0
Japanese and Japanese	18	Japanese and Japanese	50
Nisei	1	Nisei	0
Non-Japanese	1	Non-Japanese	0
Total	100	Total	100
(N)	(83)	(N)	(62)

Source: "New Leaders in the Americas," *Seikyo Times*, April 11, 1966, pp. 10 and 24.

(N) = number of cases on which percentages are based.

Japanese names, while in another four, the husband was apparently an American and the wife a Japanese. In South America, twenty (32 per cent) of the leaders were husband and wife teams.[31]

Finally, in Table 3 we have the evidence from our analysis of all overseas Sōka Gakkai members mentioned in the *Seikyō Shimbun* from 1960 to 1965, a total of 2,063 persons. According to this, the overseas members were predominantly females, and of Japanese national origin. The only apparent exceptions to this were in South America where males predominated, and in Southeast Asia where we were not able to determine from the *Seikyō Shimbun* accounts the sex of half of the

[31] We do not have such complete information on the names of leaders in other overseas areas, but an article in the *Seikyo Times*, February 11, 1966, pp. 2–3, reported on promotion examinations given by the Study Department in the Philippines and in France. In the Philippines, 56 members took the test: 55 per cent in Japanese, 43 per cent in English and 2 per cent in Tagalog. In France, 40 members took the test: 55 per cent in Japanese, 32.5 per cent in French and 12.5 per cent in English. Thus here, too, Japanese seem to comprise the majority of the membership.

TABLE 3

Sex, National Origin, and Location of the 2,063 Overseas Sōka Gakkai Members Mentioned in "Seikyō Shimbun," 1960–65

(In Per Cent)

	North America	South America	Southeast Asia	Europe	Other	Total	(N)
Sex							
Male	31	60	24	40	34	35	(732)
Female	69	40	25	60	66	56	(1,153)
No response	...	...	51	...	...	9	(178)
Nationality							
Japanese	83	99	36	61	94	79	(1,626)
Non-Japanese	17	1	64	39	6	21	(437)
National Origin							
Japan	35	96	26	63	57	46	(946)
Overseas	65*	4	74	37	43	54	(1,115)
Total	58	17	17	5	3	100	
(N)	(1,206)	(351)	(341)	(112)	(53)		(2,063)

* 2 no response.

(N) = number of cases on which percentages are based.

persons. In Southeast Asia also, more of the members were of non-Japanese than of Japanese origin.

We also see from this table that one half of all overseas members mentioned in the *Seikyō Shimbun* were in North America, mainly in the United States, and that South America and Southeast Asia together accounted for another third. Thus, the number of members in Europe, Africa, Oceania, and elsewhere is probably less than 10 per cent.

The Sōka Gakkai in the United States, which is the largest of the Sōka Gakkai's overseas organizations if Okinawa is included with Japan, is thus primarily a Japanese-oriented and Japanese-run organization. Since this is the case, what kind of Americans join the Sōka Gakkai, and why do Americans join it? We will explore these two questions in our next chapter.

II
AMERICAN
MEMBERS
OF THE
SŌKA GAKKAI

"I HAVE READ in the papers that the Sōka Gakkai is convert-ing many Americans," a person in America wrote a Christian missionary in Japan in 1962. "It looks like they are getting more of us than we are of them." [1] What are the appeals, both for Japanese and American members, of the Sōka Gakkai? The purpose of the next two chapters is to describe and analyze the sociopsychological characteristics of American and Japanese members of the Sōka Gakkai; to compare the characteristics of members of the two groups, and to compare the character-

---

[1] While we do not intend to discuss fully the question of who is con-verting whom the most, we should point out that Christians, though less than 1 per cent of the total population of Japan, and 3 per cent of Tokyo, are the second largest voluntary-membership religious group in Tokyo, behind the Sōka Gakkai. About three fourths of all Japanese be-long to no religious organization. Hayasaka shows that, in his study, Christians are the group most frequently mentioned by those of no religion in response to the question, "If you were to join a religion, which would it be?" Tajirō Hayasaka, *Shinkō Shūkyō ni Kansuru Shakai Shinri-gaku-teki Kenkyū* (Tokyo: Mimeographed at Rikkyō University, 1965), p. 69.

TABLE 4

CHARACTERISTICS OF 200 AMERICAN MEMBERS OF THE SŌKA GAKKAI
ACCORDING TO TESTIMONIALS IN THE "SEIKYO NEWS"
(In Per Cent)

Sex
  86 male
  14 female

Age
  66 known (10–19, 2; 20–29, 44;
  30–39, 35; 40–49, 14; 50 or
  more, 5 = 100)
  34 unknown

Race
  74 known (White, 67; Nisei, 18;
  Negro, 12; other, 3 = 100)
  26 unknown

Marital Status
  55 known (Japanese wife, 77;
  other married, 13; single, 10
  = 100)
  45 unknown

Who Converted
  60 known (wife, 63; girl friend,
  8; mother, 2; friend, 23;
  neighbor, 4 = 100)
  40 unknown

Year Converted
  65 known (1956–60, 18; 1961,
  21; 1962, 24; 1963, 26; 1964,
  10; 1965, 1 = 100)
  35 unknown

Previous Religion
  37 known
    48 Christian (Catholic, 27;
    Baptist, 11; Methodist, 5;
    Lutheran, 1; Church of
    Christ, 1; Missionary Alli-
    ance, 1; Congregational,
    1; Episcopal, 1 = 48)
    43 vague ("Christian," 23;
    "Protestant," 10; "Many
    Christian," 10 = 43)

Previous Religion (*Continued*)
    5 Buddhist (Nembutsu, 3;
    Jodo, 2 = 5)
    4 Atheist
    ———
    100
  63 unknown

Occupation
  56 military
    14 "Military"
    9 Army ("Army," 4; En-
    listed, 1; Sergeant, 4 = 9)
    38 Navy ("Navy," 32; Sea-
    man, 3; Petty Officer, 3 =
    38)
    34 Air Force ("Air," 10;
    Airman, 15; Sergeant, 9
    = 34)
    5 Marine Corps ("Marine,"
    4; Sergeant, 1 = 5)
    ———
    100
  14 civilian male
  14 civilian female
  17 unknown male

Location
  41 military (Yokosuka, 34;
  Tachikawa, 17; Yokota, 13;
  Atsugi, 8; Misawa, 7; Itazuke,
  4; Iwakuni, 2; Sasebo, 2;
  Johnson, 2; Fuchu, 2; Otaru,
  2; Okinawa, 5; Europe, 2 =
  100)
  47 U.S., civilian or military
  (California, 46; Chicago, 17;
  Hawaii, 16; D.C.—Virginia,
  5; New York, 4; Washington,
  3; Kentucky, 3; St. Louis, 2;
  Georgia, 2; Carolina, 1 =
  100)
  6 Japan, civilian
  5 unknown

istics of Tokyo members with those of a sample of Tokyo citizens.[2]

In order to understand the image of American Sōka Gakkai membership as projected by the society's media themselves, we surveyed all the copies of the Sōka Gakkai's official English-language newspaper, the *Seikyo News*, available to us (114 of 148 issues, or 77 per cent) from its first issue on May 15, 1962, to its last issue of September 28, 1965.[3] During its three-year existence, the paper generally ran four pages each issue (very rarely six) and page three was usually given over to testimonials, often with photographs and complete names and addresses, describing the lives of the American members of the Sōka Gakkai. These testimonials were either third-person descriptions written in relatively good "Japanese-English," or first-person statements apparently by the members themselves. Our examination of the 114 issues yielded exactly 200 testimonials of American members.[4]

Demographic Characteristics

Table 4 shows the characteristics of the Americans which were extracted from the testimonials contained in the *Seikyo News*. From the data there, we are led to conclude that the "typical" American member is a white male in his twenties or thirties,[5] in the military but of less than officer rank, married

[2] We originally planned a similar comparison of the American Sōka Gakkai members with a sample of American military personnel in the Kanto Base Command, but our study was prohibited by the American military the very evening interviewing began.

[3] The *Seikyo News* was superseded by the now weekly magazine, *Seikyo Times*, and by the first bimonthly (August, 1964), then weekly (April, 1965), and now thrice-weekly (August, 1965) *World Tribune*.

[4] We omitted in our collection testimonials from Japanese, other Asians, Europeans, or other foreigners. However, testimonials from American citizens made up about 90 per cent of all those included in the *Seikyo News*.

[5] The actual age of the members is not quite as accurately known as is indicated here. The actual age was given for only 57 (28 per cent) of the members, and we simply estimated the age of the rest from the photographs that accompanied the articles. The actual age distribution was: teens, 5 per cent; twenties, 56 per cent; thirties, 21 per cent; forties, 14

to a Japanese who was a member of the Sōka Gakkai before they met, converted by his wife, and (though here we are on very shaky ground because most testimonials did not give data concerning this) of Roman Catholic or lower-class Protestant background. Most American members were converted in the three years between 1961 and 1964. They were assigned to military facilities in the Kantō area of Japan, one third coming from the naval station of Yokosuka, near Yokohama, while the two air bases of Tachikawa and Yokota, in metropolitan Tokyo, accounted for another one fourth. In the United States, nearly half of the members were in California, with one sixth each in Chicago and Hawaii.

Fifty-six per cent of the American members were in the military, with the Navy and Air Force predominating. There was not a single commissioned officer identified as such in the testimonials. The occupation of 17 per cent of the members was not given, while 14 per cent were male civilians. The occupations of the civilians were: two teachers, two managers, four entertainers, four engineers, three salesmen, three mechanics, one carpenter, four laborers, one truck driver, two janitors, and one identified as a director of a jujutsu school.

Fourteen per cent of the members were female civilians, but five women were military dependents (four wives and one daughter), and the occupations of nineteen women were not given. Of the remaining three, one was a teacher, one a legal secretary, and one a steam-press operator.

While two thirds of the members were white, it is significant to note that Nisei and Negro account for about one sixth each of the membership. Most group photographs of Sōka Gakkai meetings show at least one male Negro.[6]

---

per cent; and fifties, 3 per cent. The range was from 8 to 58, with the median known age being 27. Thus, our estimate may slightly overstate the number of persons in their thirties and understate those in their twenties. It would be safest to assume that most members from whom we have testimonials are in their late twenties and early thirties.

[6] One Negro member of the Sōka Gakkai has been especially active in trying to encourage American Negroes to join. He has written one article that appeared in the *Negro Digest*, September, 1964, and perhaps others as well. Another Negro, writing in the *Seikyo News*, had this to say: "I believe as a member of Sokagakkai American Headquarters and moreover as a citizen of the United States that we should achieve in

Probably the most significant finding concerning the characteristics of Sōka Gakkai members is that about three fourths of those on whom we have data concerning marital status are males who are married to Japanese Sōka Gakkai members, and that nearly as many specifically said they were converted by their wives.

Contents of the Testimonials in the Seikyo News

Almost all of the testimonials centered on accounts of the subjects' troubled lives before entrance into the Sōka Gakkai, the events which led them to join that organization, and subsequent "divine benefits" that they had received. Generally, the problems that the members encountered before joining were in one (or all) of three areas: *sickness* (including both mental and physical distresses) was mentioned by 57 per cent of the members, *financial problems* were cited by 28 per cent, while problems of *human relations,* especially domestic squabbles and the lack of friends, were mentioned by 18 per cent.[7]

The most frequent specific difficulty expressed in the testimonials of American members was drinking. Fourteen per cent of the persons, all males, mentioned that they had problems in this area. Following are some extracts from the testimonials concerning drinking.[8]

He used to drink excessively causing continuous family troubles. [White, 43, Navy, Methodist, No. 15]

He would drown grief and pain in drink, which all the more drove him to a miserable life. [White, 23, Marine, Methodist, No. 13]

---

wall-to-wall Shakubuku and introduction of True Buddhism to the Negroes for a better life filled with kudoku, divine benefits. We must oscillate more with ourselves for unity." *Seikyo News,* No. 98.

[7] Percentages totaled more than one hundred because many testimonials mentioned more than one problem.

[8] In the following testimonials, the data in parentheses after the quotations refer to race, age, occupation/military service, religion, and issue number of the *Seikyo News,* in that order, as that information was available. All are male, unless otherwise indicated. Spelling, grammatical, and other errors in the testimonials have not been corrected.

He drank heavily and often fought with others under the influence of alcohol. Mr. P. was even court marshaled for injuring his superior after drinking heavily. [White, 27, Airman, Missionary Alliance, No. 20]

He would drink excessively and not return home, indulging in all the vices connected with this type of life. [White, 20's, Army Sergeant, Baptist, No. 23]

The local bar and hottle occupied his seven nights a week and he began to black out, whereas for short times unable to give an account of his actions. [Negro, 20's, Army Sergeant, Catholic, No. 26]

Japan was not such paradise as he had heard about, so he started on the bottle and having the troubles of a single man. [Negro, 20's, Airman, No. 32]

He always searched in vain for an answer to his problems but found that since he was a strict Christian, he could never discover a solution and always ended up in a bar drinking his troubles away, feeling sorry for himself. [White, 30, Navy, Catholic, No. 38]

I was released from the hospital after being treated for alcoholism—this was my second such stay in such the hospital. Thus I came to Japan determined to stay sober. I succeeded to a degree through the use of will power. However, each day was a struggle. I was never really without the urge for alcohol. [White, 40's, civilian, Jew, No. 89]

After Korea, I was sent to Japan where I became the king of the drunkards. [White, 30's, Marine, Lutheran, No. 144]

Thirteen per cent of the members stated that they had some sort of "mental" weakness, ranging from schizophrenia to extreme timidity and shyness. Illnesses of their wives were the third most frequently mentioned health complaint, given by 11 per cent of the American members. Of these difficulties, those pertaining to childlessness, or, conversely, problems relating to pregnancy or childbirth, were most frequent. Similarly, five of the members mentioned some illness which their children had.

The core section of the testimonials, however, was the

recitation of the divine benefits that the subjects had received from the Gohonzon since becoming members. As the sum of the percentages above would show, 70 per cent of the members mentioned a health, financial, or human relation problem which they had had before entering the Sōka Gakkai and which had subsequently been eliminated. In addition, 25 per cent of the members stated that they had received some divine benefit, but did not specify what their prior complaint had been. Only 5 per cent of the testimonials failed to mention that the member had received divine benefits since joining the Sōka Gakkai, but these articles were almost entirely those that enumerated the merits of Nichiren Shōshū over other forms of religion, though not mentioning any particular benefit that the member in question had received.

Since virtually all the testimonials recounted divine benefits, we shall note below a few which we feel not only are typical of the rest, and of the format of the testimonials generally, but also will enable us to point out other aspects of American membership in the Sōka Gakkai:

I became a convert, for a very simple reason: This religion does work here and now, not in some possible after-life. All one has to do is believe, pray to the Gohonzon morning and night, and the results are fabulous. [White, 49, English teacher, No. 38]

I began to chant the Daimoku praying for her quick recovery. In fact, her doctor said he had never seen any one who recovered so fast. This gave me the first actual proof. After that I prayed more and more. [Negro, 30's, Airman, Protestant, No. 55]

Recently, I received proof of Gohonzon's power and protection, when I fell from a high ladder while working. Although I should have landed on the pipes below me, surely sustaining injury, I somehow missed them and landed on the floor. As I lay on the floor not knowing what injury I had sustained, I gave Daimoku with the Dai-Gohonzon in my mind.
Upon arising, I found to my surprise that I was not injured except for a strained knee. Later upon doing Daimoku, facing the Gohonzon, the swelling subsided and my leg is now completely sound. Now I am fully confident in Gohonzon's divine protection. [Civilian, No. 68]

The first month I noticed a change in my family life and my headache was not bothering me too often. On the second month my husband got a part-time job to help with our financial burdens and in three months we could lead a completely happy family life. I have found through actual experience when I neglect worship, my life goes back to the same situation as before. [Female, Nisei, 30's, No. 59]

The doctor told me I had symptoms of tuberculosis and that he would do a lung tap at 8:00 a.m. on Friday. I went out to Keiko's house and told her what the doctor said. All she said was, "I think you had better say Daimoku, Nam-myoho-renge-kyo." I started saying the Daimoku to the Gohonzon at about 3:30 p.m. on Thursday. Keiko joined me at about 7:00 p.m. and we continued until 7:00 a.m. Friday. At 8:00 a.m. I went back to the hospital. The lung tap was a complete failure for all the fluid that was there on Thursday was gone on Friday! The doctor wanted to know what happened. I told him I said the Daimoku to the Gohonzon all night and he wanted to know what it was all about. The doctor said that in all his forty years medical experience, he had never run across anything like that before. [White, 30's, Navy, No. 74]

I have found only one truth, only one power, only one thing constant in my life. I have found the Gohonzon, with its far reaching mercy for all people. . . . I wish to tell all people about the Gohonzon as a disciple of Nichiren Daishonin, the True Buddha. I can show the Gohonzon's power, the only constant thing to all people in all places. And the unfathomable mercy and vital life-force derived from the Gohonzon can fill their lives as it has filled mine. [Navy, No. 72]

We would like to develop seven themes that we think are suggested by these testimonials: (1) The Gohonzon is considered to be the source of all power and protection. (2) The Gohonzon is believed to offer a genuine, practical, this-worldly, and immediate solution to any problem. (3) All areas of life are considered manipulative by prayer to the Gohonzon. (4) Not only is the Gohonzon believed to grant divine benefits, but it is also thought to mete out divine punishments. (5) The power of prayer to the Gohonzon is not held dependent upon the depth or purity of the faith of the person praying. (6)

Reliance upon the Gohonzon is not said to relieve the believer of utilizing all of his own and of society's resources as well in the solution of his problems. (7) Sōka Gakkai members are led to expect resistance or persecution from nonbelievers.

1. *The Gohonzon is the source of all power.* Nichiren is said to have written his interpretation of the essence of the Lotus Sutra upon a mandala which he declared to embody his own life and thought. This is the frequently mentioned Gohonzon. Just where the original mandala (the Dai-Gohonzon) is remains a point of controversy among the Nichiren sects. As we mentioned before Nichiren Shōshū–Sōka Gakkai claims to have the original enshrined in their main temple, but the other sects, and many scholars, deny this.

Each member (actually, the first converted member of each household) receives a copy (*i.e.,* a Gohonzon) which he puts in a special place (the *butsudan,* family altar), and before which he says his morning and evening prayers (called Gongyo). The most important of these prayers is the Daimoku, the words *Nam-myōhō-renge-kyō,* in praise of the Lotus Sutra.

Nichiren Shōshū teaches that Nichiren himself is *the* Buddha, the powers of the original Indian Buddha, Sakyamuni (563–483 B.C.), having ended in the Mappō (the "latter days" of the Buddhist Law), as Sakyamuni himself is said to have predicted. The Gohonzon moreover is held to be the actual embodiment of Nichiren himself, in a doctrine of "real presence," and since Nichiren himself is the Buddha, the Dai-Gohonzon is considered to be the source of all power and truth, each separate Gohonzon sharing fully in this power. As our testimonials show, by chanting the Daimoku to the Gohonzon, all wishes will be granted.

The construction worker who fell without serious injury also mentioned that he "gave the Daimoku with the Dai-Gohonzon in my mind." Apparently he had visited Taiseki-ji and had seen the Dai-Gohonzon itself. One of the most important events in the life of any Sōka Gakkai member is a pilgrimage (called Tozan) for this purpose. The Sōka Gakkai assures that a steady flow of believers visit Taiseki-ji for this. It has built a huge hall (the Dai-Kyakuden) and several lodging quarters to house pilgrims, bought a 2,800-ton liner to carry members from southern Japan and the islands to Tokyo,[9] and encouraged overseas members in their visits.

The following quotations from the testimonials make clear the importance of Tozan in reinforcing the believers in their faith:

> But when I saw the Dai-Gohonzon, I felt something inside me that I couldn't explain. I felt something powerful while chanting the Daimoku to the Dai-Gohonzon. [White, 27, Navy, No. 41]

> It is beyond my capacity to say just what I saw and I felt. There is no words to express what I felt when I first saw the Dai-Gohonzon. [White, Navy, No. 73]

> It had a good feeling to be among so many people and chant the *Nam-myoho-renge-kyo*. [Navy, No. 73]

> At 9:30 we marched up to the colossal Dai-Kyakuden. I was so impressed with its majestic splendor that I could not keep from crying. [White, 30's, No. 74]

> Plainly speaking, about 40% of the Tozan ticket for my wife and I was unexpected benefits from the Gohonzon. [White, 30's, Civilian, "Christian," No. 75]

> I accepted Gohonzon on August 28, 1960 and made a pilgrimage to the Head Temple Taiseki-ji. I prayed before the Dai-Gohonzon asking for three things. All have been answered. [White, 30's, No. 123]

2. *Practical and immediate benefits.* As this last testimonial reminds us, and as we clearly saw in those quoted earlier, one of the greatest appeals of Nichiren Shōshū–Sōka Gakkai over other religions is that the Gohonzon is believed to provide

---

[9] The ship, the *Fuji Maru*, is said to be able to hold 1,800 passengers. Its maiden voyage was on September 24, 1965. In addition to a Butsudan for the Gohonzon and a large lecture room, there is closed circuit television for mass prayer and study purposes (see the cover photograph and article in the *Seikyō Graphic*, October 5, 1965, pp. 13–15, and an article, October 12, 1965, pp. 26–29).

According to a *Yomiuri Newspaper* report of May 23, 1966, while the ship was en route from Tokushima Prefecture to Shizuoka Prefecture with 928 Sōka Gakkai passengers, its rudder broke in a storm, and it drifted for six hours. No injuries were reported. Sōka Gakkai media apparently did not carry accounts of the mishap.

immediate and this-worldly solutions to the problems of the individual and of society. This leads us to seek to know in more detail how the American members of the Sōka Gakkai compare Nichiren Shōshū with other religions, especially with Christianity, with which so many of them apparently were at one time affiliated.

The first theme we notice is that Christianity is held to be unreasonable and unscientific:

> Mr. J. was a strong Roman Catholic and wanted to be a priest of the sect. It was because many people believe in God and there must be something powerful to save people. As his study in the Christian doctrine progressed, however, his expectation was betrayed. He could not believe in an invisible being and the Bible was too contradictory and unscientific to be trusted as the basic way of life. [White, 25, Airman, Catholic, No. 13]

> He had gone to the M. Bible Institute several years ago, and had supposedly been given "all the answers." However, when he was given the job of Youth Director of the First Christian Church at K. Texas, he found that he didn't have all the answers. One day he was asked by a lady, "How do you know there is a God? If there really is one, where is he?" This question had him stumped. How could he explain something that he wasn't sure of himself? He went to his pastor. Much to his surprise, his pastor gave him the following answer: "Just look around you. See the trees, the birds, the flowers. That is how you know there is a God." In despair he wrote to M., and asked his former professors the same question. The answers he received reminded him of a merry-go-round. Never once did they directly answer his question. This worried him even more, so he started studying his Bible and other books to see what he could find. However, he found, instead of answers, many contradictions in his Bible. [White, 25, Navy, Church of Christ, No. 44]

Nichiren Shōshū, however, is considered to be completely logical and scientific:

> He was deeply moved by the scientific reasoning of Buddhist doctrine which was clarified to him. [White, 30's Airman, No. 24]

> What was explained to him at the meeting sounded far more logical and truthful than Christianity ever did. [White, 21, Navy, No. 30]

Upon studying them I was surprised to note the logic in Nichiren Shoshu and how it embraced scientific principles, including such sound theories as the law of cause and effect. [White, 30's, salesman, No. 55]

Christianity, moreover, is seen as being intolerant, while Nichiren Shōshū is not:

I came to Japan as a missionary but became disgusted by the hypocrasy and narrow-mindedness of missionaries and contradictions of Christianity. [Nisei, 32, teacher, Protestant, No. 38]

There was a town in Montana, U.S., where I was working. On one side of the street, there was a Methodist church, and on the other side, a Baptist church. I had been to both of them from time to time. One Sunday morning, the two preachers met out in the street and they moved to the front yard of one of the chapels and had a fist fight. To me this never looked good and I never returned to either of the churches. [Airman, Protestant, No. 74]

He had another bad experience with Christianity. He and his wife were married in March, 1962 at the American embassy. A few months later he thought he would go to confession at the church. At this time his allegiance was wavered between Christianity and the True Buddhism. The priest said he was not married in the church, therefore was not married, and that he would have to stop living with "that woman" until married in the church. This time he lost faith in Christianity completely. [White, 23, Navy, Catholic, No. 29]

But the most important objection to Christianity, and the theme that runs through all of the testimonials as proof of the superiority of Nichiren Shōshū, is that Christianity is other-worldly and ineffectual, while Nichiren Shōshū is able to solve the problems of this world now:

Catholicism is not the religion for the individual, but for the church. . . . According to Catholicism, life after death is stressed, while on the other hand, Nichiren Shoshu makes much of the present life. This is the reason why I dare say Catholicism is by far inferior to Nichiren Shoshu, because nobody has ever seen life after death. Nobody ever saw hell, heaven, nor purgatory. [White, 40's, Catholic, No. 38]

More than this, Christianity is held to blame for many of the ills of this world:

> Man needs a religion and a man needs happiness. The Christian church has not produced happiness. It has produced descension, misery and poverty, war and bloodshed. [English teacher, White, No. 38]

> I was raised in my childhood by very devout parents who belonged to the United Protestant Church. Until the age of 18, I participated in all church activities and put my heart into this religion, but it seemed as if the more I tried to be a good Christian, the less I knew and the less I received from it. [White, 39, Army, Protestant, No. 38]

> Previously he was a member of the Congregational Church for 25 years, but he found out that Christianity was of little help in relieving his anxiety and tension when he was in a troubled situation. [Nisei, 43, Congregational, No. 44]

Therefore, what these members sought, and claim to have found in the Sōka Gakkai but not in Christianity, is actual proof here and now:

> I had been a Protestant from 12 years old until for some 20 odd years. I was told by my wife who had five years' experience that this religion would give me actual proof. This I wanted to experience very much. [Negro, 30's, Airman, Protestant, No. 55]

> Because of my youth and lack of exposure to any but the traditional Christian faith, I joined the Baptist Church. In order to obtain God's blessings, I worked very hard and became a Sunday School teacher, along with singing in the choir and reading the Bible from 5 to 6 o'clock every morning. During this Baptist period of about two years, I saw many things go wrong with my life. . . . Finally, after two unhappy years, I quit the Baptist Church and in its place started studying psychology and philosophy. I pursued this course for almost 10 years, during which time I gained much interesting but useless information. [Female, White, 30's, Baptist, No. 144]

> You can judge a religion only through practice. You will then discover if your religion is effective, giving you what you want. If it does not, it must be an inferior religion. [White, 20's, Airman, No. 43]

3. *The Gohonzon has power over all areas of life.* We have already cited testimonials to the ability of the Gohonzon to cure all sorts of physical diseases from warts (see *Seikyo News,* No. 23) to imminent death; relieve mental distresses; increase one's income; and improve marital and other human relations. But the Gohonzon has power over other things as well. It enables one to pass tests:

> Upon joining the Soka Gakkai and earnestly chanting the Daimoku to the Gohonzon, I was able to pass a civil service exam which I had been unable to pass for some time. [Nisei, Nembutsu, No. 53]

> I prayed for a test for a navy service school which I received, I prayed that I would pass my test for petty officer first class. My wish was granted. [Navy, No. 70]

The Gohonzon is also said to be able to control the weather:

> It has been said that as the Sokagakkai membership increases in Japan, the unusual weather in that country tends to diminish in proportion to its growth. *Myoho* really means inexplicable law of the universe. When millions of Americans accept the Gohonzon and start to chant *Nam-myoho-renge-kyo,* I am sure we shall see less rain storms, hurricanes, and inclement weather. [Nisei, 43, Congregational, No. 140]

> [Under a headline, "Members in Minnesota Unaffected by Floods,"]: Sokagakkai members in Minnesota, however, are all safe while many people suffered damage. [White, 28, Air Sergeant, Baptist, No. 127]

Japanese-language media of the Sōka Gakkai stress that the Gohonzon has power to prevent accidents,[10] reduce earthquakes, fires, floods, and other disasters,[11] and, through the

[10] The *Seikyō Graphic,* February 13, 1964, pp. 12–14, has figures on automobile accidents in Japan during January, February, and March, 1963, which show that while members of other religions have a high proportion of fatalities, there are none among Sōka Gakkai members. Three testimonials from Sōka Gakkai members who were in accidents but who were spared from serious injury are also given.

[11] There have been a number of articles in the *Seikyō Graphic* which state that this is the case, especially concerning typhoons. Both the January 1, 1964, and February 25, 1965, issues have accounts which state that typhoons are fewer and less severe where Sōka Gakkai members live, or in years following major advances made by the Sōka Gakkai. Typhoons are said to be worse, however, in areas where other religions predominate.

placing of Sōka Gakkai members in positions of governmental authority, guarantee a tranquil and peaceful society, for both Japan and the world. Although these themes have occasionally appeared in the *Seikyo News*, they did not appear in the American members' testimonials we collected, save for the two items concerning the weather, given above, and one brief mention of world peace:

> Since Gohonzon possesses the power to alleviate hardships, cure sicknesses, reform one's character, and provide true material and spiritual happiness, there can be no doubt that it has the power to bring about world peace. [Nisei, civilian, No. 110]

4. *Divine punishment.* Not only does the Gohonzon bestow blessings upon believers, but it is also said to mete out divine punishment on those who do not believe, and on those who lapse in faith. The present president of the Sōka Gakkai, Daisaku Ikeda, presented the official position as follows:

> A person who slanders the Gohonzon purposely or inadvertently will surely bring retribution upon himself. We suffer miserable lives because we spoke ill of the Gohonzon in the past. . . . Those who have looked askance at believers in the Gohonzon will became blind or cross-eyed. If we have faith in a heretical religion . . . , we will have weak eyes or become short-sighted. In the light of the Law of Cause and Effect, we can clearly trace this back to the main cause of these phenomena.
>
> A pugnose is the result of slander. A person whose nose is hidden in profile suffers retribution for his slandering of a believer in the Gohonzon. When he abuses true believers, the breath will have influence on the teeth. Excessively thick, ugly lips and malocclusion comes from the same cause.
>
> The lame are no exception. A person with twisted limbs must have kicked believers who had faith in the Gohonzon, hence the deformed arms and legs.
>
> Leprosy and asthma are also retributions of slander. To be afflicted with a ceaseless cough is regarded as proof of slander in the past. Peritonitis, pyaemia, and diseases with offensive odors are explained in the sacred scriptures. There are also many other serious illnesses. Among these are included stupidity and perverseness throughout one's whole life. In spite of their endeavors, some people live unhappily, distressed with family discord such as divorce

and other troubles. Shortage of money may be also included among the serious diseases.

In order to live a happy life, solving these problems, surmounting all hardships and changing our destinies, we must worship the Dai-Gohonzon with ardent faith. . . . We cannot be happy unless we worship the Gohonzon.[12]

Testimonials showed how this was thought to operate, before they became members, in their own lives:

On March 8, 1963, I was cleaning some paint brushes with toulene, a highly inflammable fluid, comparable to gasoline. After I had finished cleaning them, I had to pass by a burning barrel of trash, in order to dispose of the toulene. A flying spark ignited the can of toulene. I threw the cans of burning fluid away from me, spilling it over my hands and forearms. I crossed my arms against my chest and pressed them under my armpits in an effort to smother the flames on my hands. I was then able to put out all the flames by rolling in the dirt on the ground. . . . My wife was already a believer in the Nichiren Shoshu Buddhism, and since our marriage in August of 1959, she had been trying to convert me. I had strongly resisted all her efforts and had threatened to burn her "black box" and its contents. I would say that I'd burn it with kerosene or something similar, and she would protest by saying that if I said such things, someday I, myself, would be burned in the same manners. [No. 140]

More frequent, however, were accounts of what happens when members lapse in faith or become careless about their prayers:

This is when he became over confident, cockey as some people put it. He felt as though he could do no wrong and as though the world were in the palm of his hand. This was the beginning of the downfall. He stopped going to meetings, as he felt that he had his life under control. Finally, he lost his job, family, and all of his friends. [White, 30's, No. 27]

Due to his good fortune following conversion to Nichiren Shoshu, he became self-satisfied and began to ignore the religion. He was ordered to go to Taiwan and henceafter he gradually came to neglect his daily chanting of the Daimoku. He stopped writing to

[12] Daisaku Ikeda, *Lectures on Buddhism* (Tokyo: Seikyo Press, 1962), I, 108–10.

his wife in Japan, his relations with friends and on the jobs became very bad, and he started having trouble with the marriage papers. From the letters he received from his wife, he realized that these troubles were due to his neglect of religious activity, and so began to concentrate again on Daimoku and Shakubuku. His worries disappeared; he again picked up with his friends and on the job. [White, 23, Marine Sergeant, Christian, No. 31]

I began to feel that I could have accomplished all these favors without the help of the Gohonzon. I stopped practicing the religion and became very conceited. Then my thoughts led me to a point of confusion and frustration. I could no longer find contentment with anything that I did. So I began to drink. Several times while on a wild ride in the car, I was stopped by policemen. But each time I was only warned. This made me even more conceited. Things went that way as long as my wife contined to pray for my safety and good luck. One evening three months later, my wife became thoroughly disgusted with me and prayed only for her own happiness. The following morning I awoke in jail. . . . I was seriously contemplating suicide. . . . Then my wife reminded me that I still had the Gohonzon. . . . So I set myself to chanting the Daimoku and practicing Gongyo and Shakubuku. After two months, I had my record of conviction expunged. . . . I began to enjoy life again. Now I realize that I have experienced divine favor and divine punishment. I no longer have any doubts about the power of the Gohonzon. [Military, Christian, No. 60]

If one is regular in his prayers and participates fully in Sōka Gakkai activities, all will be well:

Since then she has prayed to the Gohonzon earnestly. At present it is her habit to do Gongyo in the morning before going to school. She knows that if she neglects the Gongyo, everything does not go smoothly all day long. [Female, 13, military dependent, No. 45]

When I wake up in the morning the first thing I do is recite the morning sutras, and chant as much Daimoku as possible. I do this because I know when I fail to do so, or put off Gongyo till a little later, everything does not run smoothly. It seems as if I'm out of touch with the universe and this world. [White, 30's, Navy, No. 55]

5. *Reluctant or ignorant acceptance.* We saw before that the power of the Gohonzon is not held to be dependent upon

the purity or depth of faith of the believer. The Daimoku has power even when the person saying it has doubts about its efficacy. Indeed, a surprisingly large number of the testimonials relate how the subject at first did not believe in the Gohonzon, but only chanted it to quiet his wife or to test it out. Then, after receiving actual proof of divine benefit, he came to believe:

> Unable to bear hardship any longer, Kazumi accepted the Gohonzon, but with the condition that unless she obtained actual proof of its power within 100 days she would discard faith. [Navy, No. 24]

> He said to her, "You should try. If anything does not happen within 100 days, you may give up." At first, she was afraid but decided to follow his words. [Female, White, 30's, military housewife, Baptist, No. 49]

Frequently they admitted that they knew nothing about the religion when they joined it:

> I joined this religion for the sole reason that I didn't have anything else to believe in. Although I didn't know anything about it except how to chant the Daimoku, much to my suprise, good things started happening to me. [White, 20's, Navy, No. 38]

> I accepted this religion not because I believed in it but because I promised I did not have to give up my previous religion until I was really convinced. [Negro, 30's, Airman, Protestant, No. 55]

> At first H. did not find himself believing in the Buddhism because he considered Gohonzon a mere scroll of paper. Even after he married Sachiko, who first introduced Gohonzon to him, he wondered why his wife would sit in front of a piece of paper and pray everyday. . . . His wife persuaded him to chant Daimoku, Nam-myoho-renge-kyo, for a week without fail. He recalled later: "I tried to chant Nam-myoho-renge-kyo for the first time then. Then my prayer became more and more eager until one day my prayer was answered." [22, Catholic, No. 112]

The more common "reluctant acceptance" was to end the insistent pressure from a wife or friend:

> Finally, just to quiet her from talking about the Gohonzon all the time, he faced the Gohonzon and chanted the Daimoku with-

out reverence. To him, it was still something pagan, and he was doing it without belief just to prove to her that she was wrong. To his surprise, however, he found himself not having to take the medicine for a long time. He soon realized his illness was gone. It was at this time that faith come to him, and began praying earnestly to the Gohonzon. [White, 29, Navy, Christian, No. 29]

B. thought his wife foolish. She would attend the meeting of the Sokagakkai very frequently. This made him angry at times. Her only answer was that his attitude was such because he didn't know the wonderful power of the Gohonzon. [Negro, 20's, Christian, No. 31]

She insisted on making him a believer in the Gohonzon, and at last he came to think seriously of it. Quite contrary to his intention, he was converted to the teachings of Nichiren Daishonin in February 1961. The main reason he accepted this religion was to stop his fiance and other people from badgering him about it. But this didn't change his mind to the faith, and he refused to pray. But one day he started really praying when he wished to see what prayer could do for them. He soon felt a change in his feelings toward everything. He gradually came to see the bright side of things; he prayed hard for promotion and in January of this year he became an airman first class, despite heavy competition. [Negro, 20, Airman, No. 32]

Notwithstanding the existence of "reluctant acceptance," the Sōka Gakkai stresses that personal experience is necessary in order to really understand the power of the Gohonzon. Mere intellectual study of Nichiren Shōshū is useless, they insist:

Only through personal experience can you feel the Gohonzon's power within your mind and body. [Female, Nisei, 30's, No. 59]

6. *The necessity of self-help.* While the Gohonzon is said to be all-powerful, the believer must also exert himself, take all normal precautions, and obtain all usual help:

However, one must also expend his own effort. If one is sick, he should make use of the doctor or if one desires something valuable he must work for what he wishes. [Mr. O]

I agree one must also work for his own happiness. I did not mean to imply that happiness will fall out of the sky. When one has reached this point, when nothing else will work, then the Daimoku is the answer. [Mr. L]

When we practice Shakubuku, we do not tell them not to go to a doctor. Doctors are very important and they can help you a lot, but what the Daimoku can really help is that when people don't have the power to do anything the Daimoku gives them the vitalistic energy to stand up and do something. [Miss K. Three excerpts from a round-table discussion, No. 90, p. 4]

Thus, the Sōka Gakkai is plainly not opposed to doctors or normal medical practice:

After all, the medication is really good today, but the power of the Gohonzon is far, far greater. [Nisei, No. 77]

The doctors gave me the best of their medical treatment to help my children. However, they had limitations. Only we who hold the Gohonzon have no limitations. [Female, Nisei, 30's, No. 85]

7. *Persecution.* The Sōka Gakkai has been the subject of an almost completely unfavorable press, both in Japan and in the United States. The *Look* article of September, 1963, was cited several times as a reason why the subject was led to join the Sōka Gakkai. But more importantly, American servicemen have been subject to pressure not to join the Sōka Gakkai. Indeed, most ordinary American servicemen with whom we have talked about the Sōka Gakkai in Japan are convinced that the Sōka Gakkai is a Communist organization. Inquiring where they might have gotten this notion, we were told that their chaplains and superior officers have publicly made this allegation.

While we have no firm evidence that this is actually the case, our discussions with chaplains and higher officers in the Kanto Base Command also led us to conclude that the American military is very reluctant to concede that membership in the Sōka Gakkai is an acceptable form of religious affiliation. Officers on two occasions have asked us to provide them with information that would help them prove that the Sōka Gakkai is a subversive political organization so that American members under their command could be dismissed or transferred as security risks.

We have no information that would lead us to conclude that either the Japanese or American manifestations of the Sōka Gakkai are anything but religious organizations which honestly believe that religion can and should affect all of a person's life and all of society, including politics. Moreover, we are not convinced that the Sōka Gakkai is in any way connected with or financed by the Communists, and we know of no reputable Japanese observer—no matter how opposed he may be to the Sōka Gakkai—who would allege that the Sōka Gakkai is Communist-oriented. Indeed, the usual Japanese accusation is that the Sōka Gakkai is a fascist organization. We have great reservations about using this label as well.

As a consequence, it is not surprising that some of the testimonials show that the American Sōka Gakkai members have been subject to considerable ridicule and "persecution":

To see his conversion, people around him were very surprised. They thought of him as the last man to have strong faith in any religion. He himself was a bit embarassed at first. . . . He was even nicknamed "Buddha Boy" by his friends. [White, 27, Airman, Missionary Alliance, No. 20]

But while still on duty, he was told he could not get a few days liberty which he needed very badly, so he went to the Chaplain to seek his help. He returned to his section with the words of the Chaplain still ringing in his ears: "I know many men like you. You don't want early liberty to find a job. You only want to go over and lay in bed with some girl; I don't approve of marriage to these girls. The only reason they marry Americans is because they have had so many abortions and diseases that they are afraid of the same thing happening again." Revolted, he discarded the Christianity and went to the Gojukai ceremony in May of 1962. [White, 23, Navy, Catholic, No. 29]

My life wasn't all roses, however. My first sergeant called me in one day to counsel me. He accused me of being weak willed in allowing my wife to convert me to Buddhism. He tried to convince me that Air Force Investigators had found Communistic financial backing in the Sokagakkai, and as soon as they could prove it, all American servicemen who were affiliated would be suspect. He called me anti-American traitor not worthy to serve in the armed services. He vowed that if war broke out he could never trust me to fight by his side. However, the very strength of his attack and the absurdity of his charges served to deepen my faith and strengthen my resolve to prove to my countrymen the value and power of Nichiren Shoshu. I was not alone in this persecution. All of us had felt it at one time or another, but I can see clearly how this persecution by ignorant Air Force officers and friends, greatly strengthened the faith of the foreign group and brought us closer together. My future was secure. I knew then, beyond a shadow of a doubt, that the sole supreme power of the universe is *Nam-myoho-renge-kyo*. [White, 20's, Airman, No. 41]

Unless you take the advice of the people who know how to create a good public image, know the moods of this country [the United States] and the personalities of this country, then this beautiful life-giving philosophy of Nichiren Daishonin is doomed to live and grow only for a short time and then wither and die. You will say that we Americans are to slow in doing our part—this is perfectly true for two reasons: remember that all the information and directions . . . are written in Japanese, this is one small reason. The main reason we are slow is because we are like a voice in the woods—no one will listen. We have not turned against our members regardless of the insults of neighbors whether they be direct or implied instead we are still trying because we know it is good, it works and we don't want to lose it. Now think of this and ask yourself who has the faith you or we the English speaking members? What persecution have you received? How much of the teachings of your Mother and Father whether they be right or wrong have you turned your back on? I say again what I have said before: I believe the Nichiren Daishonin has given me many benefits and I shall believe in Gohonzon until the day I die. [A Letter to Japanese Members, *Seikyo News*, No. 82, p. 2]

American Members of the Yokosuka Chapter

We conclude from our analysis of data in the *Seikyo News* that the typical American members of the Sōka Gakkai are white males in their twenties or thirties, in the military but not officers, married to Japanese members of the Sōka Gakkai, and converted by them. From their testimonials we would also conclude that they are relatively poorly educated and quite willing to place their faith in anything that will guarantee sudden, effortless, and total relief from their various ills and anxieties. Many of them joined the Sōka Gakkai not out of faith in its teachings but only to quiet their wives. They became true believers only after experiencing what they interpreted as being divine benefits from Gohonzon.

We were interested in seeing whether our image of the Sōka Gakkai as gained from the *Seikyo News* was a faithful reproduction of the actual American member. Thus our English-speaking Japanese research assistant, Koichi Niitsu, in July of 1964 joined an American chapter of the Sōka Gakkai located in Yokosuka, Japan. From his reports, and over twenty hours of taped sessions which he brought back for our analysis, we conclude that, at least for this group (apparently the largest foreign chapter in Japan), the description of the American members is accurate.

Yokosuka city is located about twenty-five miles southwest of Tokyo, immediately adjacent to the city of Yokohama. Foreign influence in this area is great because it has served as a major port for many years. Especially noteworthy is the fact that Yokosuka was the site of one of the principal bases of the old Imperial Navy, and naval personnel and persons connected with shipbuilding and related industries formed a major part of the prewar population. In 1945 Japan was stripped of its military forces, but Yokosuka became and has since remained an important base for the United States Navy. Moreover, when the Japanese Self-Defense Force was set up in 1952, Yokosuka became a major base for the Maritime Self-Defense Force and the site of the Japanese Self-Defense Academy.

Thus we can see that the economy and social structure of Yokosuka has for some time been affected by and geared to the needs of military personnel. In 1965, for example, 28 per cent of the working population in Yokosuka was in manufacturing occupations, 19 per cent in service-related occupations, and 19 per cent in wholesale and retail trade.[13]

As would be expected, there is also no shortage of eating and drinking facilities in Yokosuka. Bars, cabarets, and night clubs made 1,877,430,000 yen in 1964. The area immediately surrounding the naval base is filled with shops, bars, and inns catering to the needs of the American men. Our interest will

---

[13] This and other information about Yokosuka was kindly supplied by the Yokosuka city office.

center on these bars, and the women working in them, because practically all of the Americans converted to the Sōka Gakkai in the Yokosuka area were brought to the faith by Sōka Gakkai women working in these bars.

It was difficult to get detailed information about the women. Their rate of turnover was very great and they seemed to move about to the various places where American servicemen were located. The women we talked to in Yokosuka had also worked in bars near Sasebo in Kyūshū, and Iwakuni in Yamaguchi Prefecture, both of which were near American military bases.

The personal lives of these women were very unstable. Generally they had only a middle-school education or less. They came from low-income and broken families, and many had been married and divorced several times. Many had had abortions or illegitimate children; often they were prostitutes or were living with American servicemen. A high percentage were members of the Sōka Gakkai. They told us that they had tried one thing after another in an effort to find something that would alleviate their miseries and worries. Even after joining the Sōka Gakkai, they continued to try other remedies. Their overwhelming interest in the Sōka Gakkai was that it would cure them of their various illnesses and anxieties.

If such was the motive of the women who converted the Americans to Nichiren Shōshū, how was the Sōka Gakkai able to spread among the Americans?

Daisaku Ikeda was elected the third president of the Sōka Gakkai in May, 1960. In October, he announced his intention to convert the world to Nichiren Shōshū by beginning a program of *shakubuku* of foreigners. The effect of this drive in Yokosuka can be seen in the membership figures of the Yonegahama District, Yokosuka Chapter, of the Sōka Gakkai (Table 5). Only one American (in the United States Navy, and the husband of a Japanese Sōka Gakkai member) joined during the time Josei Toda was president, but from 1960, the number of non-Japanese members in the district has increased rapidly. We found the same rapid increase of American members in our analysis of the *Seikyo News*, above.

How was this increase of foreign members achieved? As far as the Yokosuka area is concerned, it is not too much to

TABLE 5

New Japanese and American Sōka Gakkai Members Added Annually
to the Yonegahama District (Yokosuka Chapter), 1954–64

Year	Japanese	American
1954	6	0
1955	8	0
1956	1	0
1957	4	0
1958	5	0
1959	11	1
1960	14	0
1961	24	3
1962	60	12
1963	242	157
1964	144	96

say that it was solely due to the vigorous activities of Sōka Gakkai women working in Yokosuka area bars.

We talked extensively with one woman who had worked in a Yokosuka bar and was now married to an American sailor whom she had met there. She had been previously married, very unhappily, to a Japanese, and had had a child by him. Now she was married to an American several years her junior, and was looking forward to going to the United States. She told us how bad her husband had been when she first met him. He drank continually, was always in trouble, and abused her. But eventually she converted him to Nichiren Shōshū, and now they led a moderately happy life, though she is very much concerned that he will return to the United States and leave her. She described for us how she and her Sōka Gakkai friends had converted many Americans:

You remember what was written in *Time?* Well, I'll tell you, it was true! In fact, it was worse than that! We would tell them, "Before I'll sleep with you, come on to the temple." Then, after they'd been baptized (*gojukai*), we'd leave them and they'd get mad and throw Gohonzonsama in the ditch. Or if they were real drunk, they'd take it on board and throw it in the harbor when they sailed away.

But I'll tell you, it's difficult to convert foreigners! For example, you know, when I'd have to go away for a couple of days, and

by the time I'd come back he [her husband] would have for-
gotten all about it, or else, because he thought it was pretty, he'd
hang it [Gohonzon] in the doorway for a decoration. He was
impossible! [Translated from an interview tape recorded at Yokosuka, October 9, 1964]

Another woman also told how she converted Americans:

We couldn't speak English very well, but we'd stand on the
street corner and say something like "Haro-san, Haro-san! Tempo
[temple], come wiz me!"

They won't let you do that any more now, but we got a lot of
members that way then. That showed how hard we tried. [Trans-
lated from an interview tape recorded at Yokosuka, October 18,
1964]

Why did these women engage in *shakubuku* in this unusual
way? Divine favor was their basic aim, and the leaders told
them that if they wanted to gain benefits, then they must perform *shakubuku*. They were told that not only would they
thus benefit themselves and others, but in the process they
would be helping bring about a truly happy, peaceful, and
prosperous world.

To further encourage *shakubuku*, the number of new households joining each month in each district was listed in the
Seikyō Shimbun, and leading districts were featured and rewarded by the Central Headquarters. Conversions were generally slow at the beginning of the month, but by the end,
"*shakubuku* pressure" would build up, and conversions would
be more frequent. Certain months were also declared to be
special "*shakubuku* months" and conversion activities were
especially vigorous then. Finally, as we have suggested before,
it was through *shakubuku* that a person gained esteem from
his fellow members. The members who were most successful
were the most highly evaluated by their peers. Thus these
women, who so desperately wanted happiness and recognition, would energetically use the only means they had to get
new members into the Sōka Gakkai. They were quite successful.

We were able to examine several thousand *gojukai* (baptism) certificates from the Nichiren Shōshū temple in Yoko-

suka. On each certificate was the signature of the person baptized, his address, the signature of the person who was his sponsor, the name of the sponsor's group or district, the signature of the officiating priest, the place, the date, and the time.

Practically all of the American names were shakily written, indicating, we feel, possibly either great haste or intoxication. The sponsors were Japanese girls, and the time was generally after ten o'clock at night. Addresses were predominantly the names of American naval vessels, especially aircraft carriers, though a few gave complete American addresses. Only a few of the American names on these certificates have ever appeared in the *Seikyo News* or the *Seikyo Times*, and we suspect that the vast majority were "converted" by the process the women described to us above. Perhaps most of these Gohonzon ended up in the ditches and harbors around Yokosuka, but some must have been kept, for on many American ships there is at least one person who considers himself to be a member of the Sōka Gakkai.

This is all the Sōka Gakkai leaders hope for at this time. They frankly admitted to us that the women's methods were dubious, but they also greatly admired the fervor of their activities, which showed that the women were enthusiastic members. Moreover, that most of the Gohonzon were discarded was, they admitted, deplorable, but it was the fault of the Americans, not of the Japanese women. The Americans would be punished for their sacrilege, and the women rewarded for their efforts. But more important, some of the Americans, the leaders argued, would be truly converted. They would form a nucleus of Sōka Gakkai believers who would spread the faith over the world. By some standards, they agreed, this might seem a strange way to convert to a religion, but the leaders believed that it was one possibly effective way to achieve what only the Sōka Gakkai could bring about—a perfect world. For such an end, surely these means were acceptable!

The Sōka Gakkai members in America took a different view of this activity, however, especially after *Time* magazine gave world-wide publicity to these bar hostesses' conversion techniques. They demanded that the headquarters in Japan put an end to these activities, and the headquarters took appropriate action. From 1965 onward, foreigners were to be admitted only after a period of training and apprenticeship, and then only through one of the foreign chapters of the Sōka Gakkai.

Yokosuka apparently has the largest number of foreign Sōka Gakkai members in Japan, but in addition we were told that in the Tokyo area, Atsugi Naval Air Station and Tachikawa Air Base have 1,500 and 300 members, respectively. Because most of the people said to be Yokosuka members were at sea, it was difficult for us to estimate the size of this chapter, but the membership rolls we examined contained over three thousand names. However, none of these three chapters during the year we observed them was able to muster more than ten foreign members to any of their regular meetings, and Yokosuka generally averaged from five to eight. Three of these Americans were the leaders. Two of the three worked in the base hospital, and the third was a mechanic who worked on the ships when they came in from their cruises. None had more than a high school education and none was an officer. All were married to Japanese Sōka Gakkai women who were older than they were. The social life of these members was completely dominated by their Sōka Gakkai activities. Their only close friends were the other families in the chapter.

Since the three became very busy when the fleet was in, meetings were generally scheduled to be held regularly when the fleet was at sea. Following the Japanese pattern, meetings were held three times a week—Sunday, Monday, and Wednesday—from seven to nine in the evening, each time at a different member's house. Once a month they visited the Nichiren Shōshū temple (Hoshōji) at Yokosuka, and about once a year they held a general meeting with the Tachikawa and Atsugi chapters, with from fifty to one hundred persons attending. Usually members from other chapters in Japan, and visitors from the United States, would also attend these yearly meetings.

As we have seen, systematic attempts to convert Americans did not begin until 1960, but for several years after no formal organization was set up for foreign members. Thus at first they attended regular Japanese meetings, and had to rely upon

English-speaking Japanese—generally their wives—to explain to them what was going on (apparently none of the Americans could speak much Japanese). If a serious problem arose, the Americans would be taken to the Overseas Bureau of the Central Headquarters in Tokyo to meet with the English-speaking personnel there.

The American Chapter at Yokosuka was formally set up in 1962. The format of the American meetings in the members' homes that we observed was generally as follows. Meetings would begin with three recitations of the Daimoku (*Nam-myō-hō-renge-kyō*) and the singing of several Sōka Gakkai songs.[14] Then the English-language *Seikyo News* would be distributed. Next would be a general discussion of a variety of often unrelated topics concerning the members' work, their spouses, the day's happenings, and topics from the *Seikyo News*. Prospective members, who would generally have been brought by one of the Japanese women, would next introduce themselves. The older members would tell them about their own experiences with Nichiren Shōshū and the divine benefits they had received. The content of these testimonials was very similar to that found in the *Seikyo News*.

This pattern was somewhat different from the Japanese discussion meetings in that one person was clearly in charge of the Japanese proceedings, and the communication flow was much more closely centered around religious topics, especially methods of *shakubuku*. Frequently, Japanese members from the Overseas Bureau would come to help the American leaders during the discussion period, but generally the English ability of the Japanese advisors was so poor, and the theological knowledge of the American leaders so inadequate, that virtually no communication occurred, much to the mutual frustration of the parties.

At about nine o'clock, the American group would once

[14] The songs of the Sōka Gakkai are generally quite stirring and martial (in the manner of "Onward, Christian Soldiers" or "Christian, Dost Thou See Them on the Holy Ground?"). The songs are sung with great gusto, usually accompanied by group hand-clapping and under the direction of a leader who uses energetic but stylized gestures with a Japanese folding fan. English translations of some songs are found in Appendix IV.

again say three Daimoku, and those who wished to go would do so; the remainder (usually only two or three Americans) would stay to talk.

The monthly meetings at the Hoshōji Temple were not much different from those in the members' homes, except that, possibly due to the influence of the surroundings, the topics of discussion would stick more closely to religion. Also, there were generally from ten to twenty persons in attendance.

In conclusion, our experiences in Yokosuka thus led us to believe that the image of the average American member projected by the *Seikyo News* corresponds to the characteristics of American members in reality. But what about the Japanese members, who of course compose the bulk of all Sōka Gakkai members, both in Japan and overseas? What are their characteristics, and how do they compare with the American members, and with Japanese who are not members of the Sōka Gakkai? These are the problems to be considered in our next chapter.

III

JAPANESE
MEMBERS
OF THE
SŌKA GAKKAI

OUR DATA ON Sōka Gakkai media-projected images of the Japanese members came from the Japanese-language weekly magazine, *Seikyō Graphic*, November 11, 1962, to April 4, 1964. The *Seikyō Graphic*, which began publication in January, 1959, is a very attractive *Life*-sized magazine, the latter pages of which are generally given over to somewhat more detailed testimonials than were found in the English-language *Seikyo News*. For convenience's sake, we took the first two hundred testimonials we found in a period roughly equivalent to our American study, though it should be noted that because we surveyed all issues of the *Seikyo News*, the American portion begins half a year earlier and runs a year and a half longer than does the Japanese. However, because there were far fewer new American testimonials in the 1965 issues of the *News* than there were from 1962 to 1964 (there being an increased number of Southeast Asia and European testimonials and some new testimonials from previous members), we feel the two studies may be considered as covering approximately the same time span.

Basic Demographic Characteristics
According to the Seikyō Graphic *and Surveys*

Table 6 shows the characteristics of the Japanese members according to the testimonials of the *Seikyō Graphic*. From

TABLE 6

CHARACTERISTICS OF 200 JAPANESE MEMBERS OF THE SŌKA GAKKAI
ACCORDING TO TESTIMONIALS IN THE "SEIKYŌ GRAPHIC"
(In Per Cent)

Sex	Who Converted	Previous Religion
74 male	52 known (58 fam-	8.5 known (3.5
26 female	ily, 42 friend =	Nichiren, 3 Zen,
	100)	0.5 Nembutsu,
Age	48 unknown	0.5 Risshō
4 aged 10–19		Kōsei Kai, 1.0
19 aged 20–29	**Year Converted**	Christian =
25 aged 30–39	1 in 1950	8.5)
24 aged 40–49	1 in 1951	91.5 unknown
21 aged 50–59	6 in 1952	
3 aged 60 and	12 in 1953	**Occupation**
above	7 in 1954	40 professional
4 aged unknown	8 in 1955	11 managerial
	9 in 1956	7 office
	8 in 1957	23 small shop
Education	8 in 1958	1 agricultural
36 known (8 ele-	6 in 1959	5 laborer
mentary, 15	8 in 1960	3 housewife
middle, 18 high,	8 in 1961	4 other
59 college =	9 in 1962	6 unknown
100)	2 in 1963	
64 unknown	7 unknown	

this we would conclude that the "typical" Japanese member of the Sōka Gakkai is a college-educated male, in his late thirties or forties, and of professional occupation. Most males appear to have been converted by friends, fathers, or relatives who were not in their immediate family, while females indicated that they were converted by their husbands or mothers. Only

17 of the 200 subjects said that they had been members of some other religion before joining the Sōka Gakkai.[1]

Table 7 presents the phenomenal growth of the Sōka Gakkai

TABLE 7

GROWTH OF SŌKA GAKKAI HOUSEHOLD MEMBERSHIP, 1951–68

Year	Household Members	% Annual Increase	Japanese Population	Events
1951	5,728	. . .	84,500,000	Toda elected
1952	22,324	74	85,800,000	President
1953	73,946	68	87,000,000	
1954	164,272	57	88,200,000	
1955	303,523	47	89,276,000	
1956	491,447	38	90,170,000	
1957	768,897	35	90,920,000	
1958	1,034,731	27	91,760,000	Toda died
1959	1,287,484	19	92,640,000	
1960	1,722,475	24	93,419,000	Ikeda elected
1961	2,316,020	26	94,280,000	President
1962	3,106,301	25	95,180,000	
1963	3,968,242	22	96,160,000	
1964	5,246,458	24	97,186,000	
1965	5,500,000 (approx.)	5	98,275,000	
1966	6,100,000 (approx.)	10	99,220,000	
1967	6,500,000 (approx.)	6	100,000,000	
1968 (July)	6,618,000 (approx.)	. . .	. . .	

from 1952 (the first year for which complete membership figures were available to us) to the end of 1966. Note that, in keeping with Japanese custom, the figures refer to the number of households and not of individual believers. Thus the exact number of actual members is uncertain since the number of persons in a household may vary considerably.

When we compare Table 7 with the section "Year Converted" of Table 6, which gives the date when the subjects of the testimonials said they were converted, we must conclude that,

[1] Probably no more than 20 to 30 per cent of the Japanese population consider themselves members of a religious organization, according to data in Jōichi Suetsuna *et al.*, *Nihonjin no Kokuminsei* (Tōkyō: Shiseidō, 1961), p. 181, and our survey of Tokyo citizens, discussed below.

even though the testimonials seem to be evenly spread over the past fifteen years, actually, older members appear to be considerably overrepresented and newer converts underrepresented.

1. *Comparison of media-projected demographic characteristics of Japanese and American members.* Considering only the impressions of Sōka Gakkai membership received from the two media sources surveyed, we would conclude that both American and Japanese Sōka Gakkai members are predominantly male, but that the Japanese members are somewhat older, are of considerably higher socioeconomic status, and have been members much longer than have the Americans. While we do not have any data on the educational attainments of the Americans, the testimonials and our participant observation do not encourage us to assume that the Americans generally are of very high education, while three fifths of the Japanese members on whom we have such information state that they are college graduates. In occupation the Japanese members likewise report considerably higher status than do the Americans.

Also of great interest is the finding that while most American males were converted by their wives (63 per cent), this was not true for *any* of the Japanese males, although more of the Japanese women reported they were converted by their husbands (35 per cent) than by any other person.

The demographic image received of the American members, then, was one of young-middle-aged, lower-rank military personnel married to Japanese members of the Sōka Gakkai by whom they recently were converted. Considering the nature and details of their testimonials, they appear to be an alienated group, beset by a variety of physical, economic, and mental misfortunes, and greatly in need of an external absolute source of authority upon which they can completely rely to give meaning to their otherwise anomic lives.

The Japanese members, on the other hand, appear for the most part to be people who are quite successful in the secular world, while the Americans are not, although the Japanese were no less insistent than the Americans that their success is wholly dependent upon divine benefits from the Gohonzon.

Concerning specific problems which membership in the Sōka

Gakkai had alleviated, the Japanese were far more likely to say that they had financial problems than were the Americans (44 per cent of the Japanese, 28 per cent of the Americans), while Americans listed health problems more frequently (56.5 per cent for the Americans, 35 per cent for the Japanese). Moreover, while drinking was the most common single complaint for the Americans (14 per cent), only seven Japanese (3.5 per cent) said they had difficulties in this area.[2] Problems of human relations were almost identical for the two groups: 17.5 per cent for the Americans and 20 per cent for the Japanese.

2. *Comparison of media-projected images of Japanese members with survey data.* We do not intend to trace the themes of Japanese-language testimonials in the detail we did for the American members, but instead will compare the image of Sōka Gakkai membership projected by its media with that derived from survey research. For this comparison, we will utilize data from four surveys: (1) a survey (N = 268) by Hiroshi Suzuki (Kyūshū University) of Sōka Gakkai members in Fukuoka city, Kyūshū, 1962; (2) a survey of a part of a ward in Tokyo (N = 232) conducted by sociology students of the University of Tokyo and Tokyo Women's University, 1962; (3) a study of a two-stage sample of Tokyo residents (N = 284) in 1964 by Tajirō Hayasaka (Rikkyō University); and (4) a random sample of Tokyo residents (N = 980) which we conducted in 1965.[3]

[2] This is perhaps because drinking and drunkenness are far less likely to be negatively evaluated from a moral standpoint in Japan than in the United States and hence are not as frequently resorted to as means of escape or rebellion. However, it is significant that a brand research study comparing the purchasing habits and brand preferences of a sample of subscribers of the Sōka Gakkai's *Seikyō Shimbun* with a sample of Tokyo citizens revealed that fewer Sōka Gakkai households drink beer (26 per cent of the Sōka Gakkai members do not, compared to only 19 per cent of the non–Sōka Gakkai sample), whiskey (58 per cent to 48 per cent), or wine (62 per cent to 55 per cent), than do nonmembers, but that the consumption of Japanese *sake* is the same for both groups (37 per cent of both do not). See Burando Kabushiki Kaisha and Ichiba Chōsa Kenkyujō, *Seikyō Brand Research* (Tokyo, Mimeographed, October, 1964), p. 41.
[3] Hiroshi Suzuki, "Toshi Kasō no Shūkyō Shūdan," *Shakaigaku Kenkyū* (of Tōhoku University), No. 22 (1963), pp. 81–102, No. 23/24 (1964), pp. 50–90; Tōkyō Daigaku Shakai Gakka and Tōkyō Joshi Daigaku Shakai Gakka (Tokyo Universities), *Sōka Gakkai* (Tokyo: Mimeographed, 1963),

The Fukuoka city chapter of the Sōka Gakkai permitted Suzuki to have access to its membership rolls, which contained the names and addresses of 20,000 households. Suzuki selected three areas (a commercial district, a residential district, and a small-shop and factory district) from which to draw, by an unspecified random method, a sample of 450 members. He was able to interview 268 (60 per cent) successfully.[4] While this method resulted in a sample which might safely be considered representative of a portion of the Sōka Gakkai members in Fukuoka, apparently no sample was drawn from the ordinary citizens themselves, so we do not know how Sōka Gakkai members compare with ordinary Fukuoka citizens, save for census-data comparisons.

The Tokyo Universities' sample was drawn from a lower-income, small-factory area in Katsushika Ward of Tokyo, called Kami Hirai Machi, 3-chōme, which had a population of 1,757 households in March 31, 1962. By taking every fourth household as listed in the official List of Residents (*Jūmin Hyō*), a sample of 400 was drawn. Forty of these were randomly discarded, and 266 persons of the remaining 400 households (71 per cent) were successfully interviewed. By this method, 33 Sōka Gakkai members were contacted, comprising 11 per cent of those interviewed. The reporters warn that the area sampled should not be considered representative of either the ward from which it was drawn, nor of Tokyo itself. Indeed, it was especially chosen because it was a lower-class neighborhood and thus, the reporters thought, likely to have a higher percentage of Sōka Gakkai members.[5]

Hayasaka also used a sampling method which resulted in a moderately large number of Sōka Gakkai members, but which raises questions as to its representativeness. First, using the twenty-three wards of Tōkyō and nine neighboring cities as the universe, Hayasaka randomly chose two hundred sampling points, and then names of persons over twenty years of age from the List of Residents (*Jūmin Hyō*) of these points. By this

139 pp.; Tajirō Hayasaka, *Shinkō Shūkyō ni Kansuru Shakai Shinrigaku-teki Kenkyū* (Tokyo: Mimeographed, 1965), 113 pp.

[4] Suzuki, "Toshi Kasō no Shūkyō Shūdan," No. 22, p. 85, note 1.

[5] Tokyo Universities, *Sōka Gakkai*, pp. 25 and 101–12.

method, an initial sample of 1,983 names was collected, to whom Hayasaka mailed a short questionnaire that included an item concerning religious affiliation; 472 persons (24 per cent) returned the questionnaire. Among this group were 71 (15 per cent of the 472) Sōka Gakkai members. Considering this too few for his purposes, Hayasaka obtained a list containing the names of Tokyo subscribers to the Sōka Gakkai's newspaper, *Seikyō Shimbun*, and by an unspecified random method, chose an additional 100 names from it. He then chose a sample of 240 persons from the 401 non–Sōka Gakkai persons who mailed back the first questionnaire, carefully matching the characteristics of this group with the original 401 according to age, sex, religion, occupation, and education. He then attempted to interview this sample of 400 (160 Sōka Gakkai members and 240 nonmembers), and completed 284 (70 per cent of the 400) cases, 129 of which were Sōka Gakkai members and 155 nonmembers. He did not relate how many of this group actually interviewed were picked up in the first stage sampling, and how many were drawn from the list of *Seikyō Shimbun* subscribers, but he did warn that the *Seikyō Shimbun* subscribers were probably not wholly representative of the total Sōka Gakkai membership, very likely being more active and interested in Sōka Gakkai matters than the average member might be.[6] Moreover, while the purpose of Hayasaka's study was specifically to compare, through the use of several psychological methods, Sōka Gakkai and non–Sōka Gakkai individuals, the sampling method utilized seems to jeopardize the representativeness not only of the Sōka Gakkai members, but of the non–Sōka Gakkai group as well.

In our study we chose to use a sampling method which we considered sufficiently representative of the adult citizens of the 23 wards of Tokyo, but which resulted in a small number of Sōka Gakkai respondents (45 of 980 respondents, or 5 per cent). We decided on our method only after we were fully convinced that no other single process would result in a sample equally representative of the Sōka Gakkai membership and of the citizens of Tokyo. Using the Election Registration List (*Kihon Senkyō Jinmeibō*) made public on December 22, 1964, to de-

---

[6] Hayasaka, *Shinkō Shūkyō*, pp. 13–15.

termine the number of registered voters (5,820,694 persons total in all 23 wards) in each ward of Tokyo,[7] we decided how many names should be drawn from each ward to total a sample of 1,000. Having been warned that because of Tokyo's highly mobile population, a considerable number of persons on the Election List would have moved by the time we interviewed them in February, 1965, we actually drew 1,500 names.

After we had determined the number of names needed from each ward to assure a number of respondents proportionate to that ward's contribution to the total number of registered voters in Tokyo, we went to each ward office, and, using a table of random numbers, drew the required number of names and addresses.[8] We then were able to interview 980 persons, 65 per cent of the 1,500 names,[9] but 98 per cent of the original sample of 1,000 that we desired.

Table 8 summarizes the basic demographic data of Japanese members of the Sōka Gakkai, according to our analysis of the *Seikyō Graphic*, in comparison with the four surveys of the Sōka Gakkai, the population from which these samples were drawn, and Tokyo census or other official data from 1965.

The survey labeled "D" and "D′ " is that conducted by the present writer, "D" being the Sōka Gakkai subsample, and "D′ " the total sample. "H" and "H′ " refer to Hayasaka's study, but while "H" designates the Sōka Gakkai subjects, "H′ " is the non–Sōka Gakkai subsample only, and not the total sample. This is also the case for "T" and "T′," which designate the Tokyo Universities' study. As noted before, Suzuki's study ("S") was of Sōka Gakkai members only, so there is no non–Sōka Gakkai comparison available.

It should also be noted that all but one of the sample surveys

[7] Registration does not depend on the initiative of the citizens in Japan but is automatically performed by the government. Thus the election lists should contain the names and addresses of all adult citizens.

[8] In some wards this was relatively easy, since registered voters were numbered consecutively from one to the total number of voters in the ward. The lists in other wards, however, were grouped according to *chō* (block) or *machi* (village) within the ward, and numbered consecutively only within each such subdivision. Other wards renumbered the voters from one to fifty on each page.

[9] The range of completed interviews within each ward ran from 47 to 80 per cent, but the median was also 65 per cent.

and official data are of Tokyo (or in the case of "T," of a small
community in Tokyo), while Suzuki's study was of Fukuoka
city, Kyūshū. Thus the Tokyo official figures should not be
used to evaluate Suzuki's Sōka Gakkai sample. Also, the dates of
the various studies differ; "T" and "S" being in 1962, while "D,"
"H," and the official data are for 1965.

a. *Education and occupation.* With these variations in mind,
let us turn first to a comparison of Japanese media images with
the survey studies of the Sōka Gakkai. We observe many striking divergences. In all of the measures we have here, we note
that while the image projected by the *Seikyō Graphic* is one of
upper status, highly educated, and prosperous members, the
realities of Sōka Gakkai membership seem vastly different. Indeed, the evidence here leads us to conclude that in education
and occupation, the facts are exactly the opposite from those
projected by Sōka Gakkai media. The educational standard of
the average Sōka Gakkai member, according to these surveys, is
quite low—lower than that of the average Tokyo citizen, and
vastly inferior to that of the members whose testimonials
were displayed in the *Seikyō Graphic*.[10] Moreover, concerning
occupation, far from being predominantly professional and
managerial people, Sōka Gakkai members appear not only to
differ from the media projections, but to be of lower status occupations than is the Tokyo population generally.[11]

While the "H" and "T" studies did not report statistical tests
of the differences observed here, in our study the occupational
difference noted between Sōka Gakkai members and the total
sample was significant, by the chi-square test, beyond the .001
level, while the educational differences were significant at $>.10$.

b. *Income.* The average family income of Tokyo residents in
1963 was 66,439 yen per month, while that of laborers was

[10] The brand research study cited in footnote 2 showed that while
31 per cent of the non–Sōka Gakkai sample were university graduates,
only 17 per cent of the Sōka Gakkai sample were. *Seikyō Brand Research,*
p. 91.

[11] We also asked our respondents to give the occupations of their
fathers. Here as well, the Sōka Gakkai members underrepresented professional and shop occupations, and greatly overrepresented unskilled
laborers. In fact 45 per cent of all the respondents in our survey who
said their fathers were unskilled laborers were members of the Sōka
Gakkai.

TABLE 8

Demographic Characteristics of Japanese Sōka Gakkai Members in Comparison with Non-members and the Population of Tokyo
(In Per Cent)

		Seikyō Graphic 1962-64	Sōka Gakkai				Non-Sōka Gakkai			Tokyo Population 1964-65
			D 1965	H 1964	T 1962	S 1962	D' 1965	H' 1964	T' 1962	
Sex	Male	74	51	60		38	51	61		51
	Female	26	49	40		62	49	39		49
	Total	100	100	100		100	100	100		100
Age	20's	24	24	12	48	14	33	30	36	32
	30's	25	27	29	26	23	28	30	32	24
	40's	24	27	33	13	32	17	19	21	19
	50's plus	23	22	26	9	31	20	21	10	25
	No response	4			4		2			
	Total	100	100	100	100	100	100	100	99	100
Education	Elementary	8	18	57	65	26	12	28	50	13
	Middle	15	33	35	31	37	27	44	33	31
	High	18	36	8	0	29	43	28	16	41
	College	59	9		0	8	15			15
	No response		4		4		3			
	Total	100	100	100	100	100	100	100	99	100
Family Monthly Income (in yen)	Less than 20,000		4	30*	22	28	3	26*	10	0
	20,000–29,999		22	22	13	34	9	26	14	3
	30,000–39,999		9				13			10
	40,000–49,999		13	33	44	18	15	34	36	16
	50,000–59,999		22				12			19
	60,000–69,999		4				8			14
	70,000–79,999		0	15	9	13	5	14	16	8
	80,000–99,999		4				12			12
	100,000 plus		7		4	2	15		16	18
	No response		13	0	9	6	9	0	9	0
	Total		98	100	101	101	101	100	101	100

	(200)	(45)	(129)	(33)	(268)	(980)	(155)	(209)
OCCUPATION								
Professional	40	2	0	6	8	8	6	
Managerial	11	7	21	5	11	8	†	
Office	7	10	33	7	21	19	28	
Shop	23	24	36	38	21	20	51	
Skilled Labor		33	0	14	19	16	8	
Artisan	5	17	9	1	7	10	0	
Unskilled Labor		0		8	2	18	7	
Other	7	7			8	0		
No response	7	0			3			
Total	100	100	99	99	100	99	100	
CLASS								
Upper	2		0		10		2	
Middle	49		26		62		27	
Lower	38		57		18		62	
No response	11		17		11		9	
Total	100		100		101		100	
(N)	(200)	(45) (129)	(33) (268)	(980) (155) (209)				

(N) = number of cases on which percentages are based.

Data for "D" and "D" are from our 1965 Tokyo survey; "H" and "H" from Tajirō Hayasaka, *Shinkō Shukyō ni Kansuru Shakai Shinrigaku-teki Kenkyū* (Mimeographed, 1965), p. 16; "T" and "T" from Tōkyō Daigaku Shakai Gakka and Tōkyō Joshi Daigaku Shakai Gakka, *Sōka Gakkai* (Mimeographed, 1963), pp. 102–11; "S" and "S" from Hiroshi Suzuki, "Toshi Kasō no Shūkyō Shūdan," *Shakai Kenkyū*, No. 22, 1963, p. 89; "Tokyo Population" from *Tōkyō no Jinkō* (Tōkyō: Tōkyō Tōkei Kyōkai, 1965), p. 13; *Tōkyōto Tokubetsu-ku no Yoron Chōsa* (Tōkyō: Tōkyōto Yoron Chōsa Iinkai, 1965), p. 23.

* These figures are for *individual*, not family, income and thus are considerably lower.

† Comparable data not given, but breakdowns for three occupational categories were as follows (Hayasaka, *Shinkō Shukyō*, p. 115):

	Sōka Gakkai %	Non-Sōka Gakkai %
Category I (Laborers, Family Workers, Small Shop Workers)	49	30
Category II (Office Workers, Government Workers, Self-employed)	21	38
Category III (Housewives, Unemployed)	20	32

59,652 yen. In our survey, only 15 per cent of the Sōka Gakkai members had a monthly income, in 1965, of 60,000 yen or more. Thus the Sōka Gakkai members, in all four surveys, had incomes below those of even the average working family. The differences we found between the income of the Sōka Gakkai members and the total sample were significant at >.01.

c. *Class.* Both the "T" study and our own included measures of social class. In the Tokyo Universities' research, class was objectively determined by the analysis of a combination of items. In our study we simply asked our interviewers to indicate what they thought the class of their respondents was, and why. While our method has its drawbacks, the differences reported between Sōka Gakkai members and the total sample were significant beyond the .001 level, and are in keeping both with the differences reported in the "T" study and with the other indicators described above. That is, Sōka Gakkai members appear to be found in the lower classes more frequently than is the total population.

The *Seikyō Shimbun* brand research report indicated that, generally speaking, the purchasing habits and brand preferences of Sōka Gakkai and non–Sōka Gakkai members were largely the same, but that there were also a good many indications that Sōka Gakkai families have fewer home appliances, durable goods, and other possessions than do ordinary Japanese. The following pairs of numbers show the percentage of Sōka Gakkai (the left number) and non–Sōka Gakkai members (the right number) *not possessing* the given item: radio, 28–9; refrigerator, 20–11; vacuum cleaner, 29–20; movie camera, 43–29; camera, 54–26; mattress, 65–55; dress shirts, 17–9; neckties, 26–11; stocks and bonds, 81–71. On most other items there were no significant differences between Sōka Gakkai members and nonmembers, but on three, more Sōka Gakkai members owned the item than did nonmembers: thermos jugs, 48–64; bicycles, 47–57; and tights, 53–64. The general impression, then, is that the average Sōka Gakkai household has a somewhat lower standard of living than does that of the average nonmember.

d. *Age.* Evidence concerning the age distribution of Sōka Gakkai members is mixed. The *Seikyō Graphic* data and our study indicate that there is no great difference: Sōka Gakkai members seem to be spread evenly among all age groups. Hayasaka and Suzuki, however, both report finding considerably more older than younger persons in the Sōka Gakkai, but the Tokyo Universities' study indicated just the opposite: nearly three fourths of their Sōka Gakkai members were below forty years of age. However, the entire received sample of the Tokyo Universities' survey was younger than that of the other studies reported here, while the age distribution of Hayasaka's Sōka Gakkai and non–Sōka Gakkai members was almost perfectly reversed.

The fact of the matter probably is that the age composition of the Sōka Gakkai is in flux. Apparently the Sōka Gakkai initially appealed to and was composed of middle-aged women, but more recently many new members seem to have been youths. The change—if there has been one—may be due to the natural introduction of "second generation believers." [12] Probably more important, however, is the fact that when the present president of the Sōka Gakkai, Daisaku Ikeda, was elected in 1960 at the age of only thirty-two, there seems to have been a shift of emphasis toward more work among college-age youth. The election of Ikeda, who had been head of the Youth Division before becoming president, was probably itself an indication of a change in this direction, but Ikeda has surely been instrumental in encouraging this development.

The photographs, phonograph records, and written descriptions of Josei Toda, the second president, and the person most responsible for the tremendous post-war growth of the Sōka Gakkai, indicate to us that though Toda was an energetic and very skillful leader, he was more a "kindly uncle" (*yasashii ojisan*), with baggy pants, steel-rimmed glasses, bucked teeth, and toothbrush mustache, who would appeal especially to tradition-oriented widows and lonely middle-aged women than a person who would attract many modern Japanese youths. Ikeda, on the other hand, while surely no less an able leader than Toda, projects a more modern and conservatively debonair image. He is generally immaculately dressed, is shown to be a sturdy

[12] See the data from Hayasaka on this point, below.

family man,[13] and is a forceful and persuasive (but not, by Western standards, dynamic) speaker.

While Ikeda stoutly denies that his appeal is in any way charismatic, the almost invariable placing of his young, handsome, and smiling face as the first and largest photograph in Sōka Gakkai intramural literature, in juxtaposition with the rapt, misty-eyed countenances of persons listening to him speak, clearly indicates, we believe, that Sōka Gakkai officials are not unaware that charisma is present.

Furthermore it has been rumored that within the Sōka Gakkai at present, there is tension between the desires and interests of the older members, who have been in the Sōka Gakkai for some time, and the younger and newer members. While there has been no sign of an open break as yet, if the growth and success of the Sōka Gakkai is arrested or other difficulties beset it, there is a possibility that schism may result.

e. *Sex.* In addition to the ambiguity of our sources pertaining to the age distribution of Sōka Gakkai members, there is also conflicting evidences as to sex. Three fourths of the *Seikyō Graphic* testimonials were from men. Hayasaka also found 20 per cent more men than women Sōka Gakkai members, but his total sample was more heavily weighted toward men than is the actual Tokyo distribution, according to data based on the List of Residents. Suzuki, on the other hand, found that three fifths of his respondents in Fukuoka were females. Our study disclosed absolutely no difference between the Sōka Gakkai subsample and the total sample, or between the latter and the total population of Tokyo: the ratio of males to females was nearly one.

In summary then, according to evidence from the surveys, the Sōka Gakkai in Japan seems to be composed predominantly of lower (but not lowest) status persons. On education, the variable which we have found to correlate most closely with

[13] This image has been strongly emphasized in recent articles in several of the popular weekly women's magazines. See, for instance, "Ningen Ikeda Daisaku," *Josei Jishin,* June 22, 1964, pp. 46–50; "Watashi wa Ikeda Daisaku no Tsuma," *Josei Jishin,* June 29, 1964, pp. 64–68; "Sugai no Ikeda Daisaku to sono Kazoku," *Josei Sebun,* August 5, 1964, pp. 15–22; and the series of four articles written by Ikeda and appearing weekly in *Josei Jishin,* January 4 to January 25, 1965.

social attitudes in Japan, most Sōka Gakkai members have distinctly less formal education than does the general population. In addition, Sōka Gakkai members have lower incomes and come proportionately more from labor, artisan, and, to some extent, shop, and less from professional, managerial, and office occupations. However, we found no consistent difference between the Sōka Gakkai and nonmembers concerning age and sex, though there may be slightly more divorced and widowed people, and significantly less single persons, in the Sōka Gakkai.

3. *Comparison with other religious groups.* But how do Sōka Gakkai members compare with members of other religions? We have stated before that only 18 per cent of our Tokyo respondents said they were members of some religious organization, and 34 per cent told us they believed in God, a Supreme Being, the Law of the Universe, or the like. The most frequently named religious group was the Sōka Gakkai (5 per cent of the total, 26 per cent of those with some religious affiliation). Christians were the second most numerous (3 per cent of the total, 19 per cent of religious affiliates), while no other single religious group had more than 1.5 per cent of the total sample, or 10 per cent of those with some religion. Thus we have reduced our data to four religious groups: the Sōka Gakkai, Christians, members of the so-called "new religions" (Risshō Kōsei Kai, Tenrikyō, P. L. Kyōdan, and so forth), and members of the "traditional" old religions (Shintō and all Buddhist groups).

Table 9 gives the demographic characteristics of the four groups, in comparison with those with no religion and with all four religious categories taken together. We can see that the four religious groups are composed of persons with quite different characteristics. Except for the Sōka Gakkai, where the proportion is nearly equal, women seem to be overrepresented in the religious groups, especially among Christians, 75 per cent of whom were women. Persons who are members of some religion seem to be older than nonaffiliates generally, but there are striking denominational differences. Affiliates of the traditional religions are overwhelmingly older, and members of the new religions are somewhat older. Sōka Gakkai members are not significantly older than persons of no religion, but Christians

TABLE 9

Demographic Characteristics of the Religious Groups of the 1965 Tokyo Sample

(In Per Cent)

	No Religion	All Religions	Traditional Religions	New Religions	Sōka Gakkai	Christians	(N)
Sex							
Male	53	42	44	41	51	25	(498)
Female	47	58	56	59	49	75	(478)
Total	100	100	100	100	100	100	(976)
Age							
20–34	52	31	8	28	44	63	(471)
35 and over	48	69	92	72	56	37	(507)
Total	100	100	100	100	100	100	(978)
Marital Status							
Married	67	68	71	72	71	53	(655)
Divorced	1	3	2	0	7	3	(16)
Widowed	3	12	21	12	7	0	(48)
Single	29	17	6	16	15	44	(258)
Total	100	100	100	100	100	100	(977)

EDUCATION							
Elementary, Middle	39	47	52	66	53	12	(382)
High, University	61	53	48	34	47	88	(565)
Total	100	100	100	100	100	100	(947)
INCOME							
60,000 yen or less	57	52	36	57	82	40	(502)
Over 60,000 yen	43	48	64	43	18	60	(392)
Total	100	100	100	100	100	100	(894)
OCCUPATION							
Shop, Laborer	50	52	46	40	74	33	(482)
Professional, White Collar	41	39	43	57	19	53	(389)
Total	91	91	89	97	93	86	(871)
CLASS							
Upper, Middle	80	79	86	75	57	96	(775)
Lower	20	21	14	25	43	4	(94)
Total	100	100	100	100	100	100	(869)
(N)	(806)	(172)	(63)	(32)	(45)	(32)	(978)

(N) = number of cases on which percentages are based.

are strikingly younger than any other religious group or than our nonreligious respondents.

There also seem to be great differences in marital status. Though the percentage of married persons is the same between religious and nonreligious persons generally, there are considerable differences between the comparative numbers of single and widowed persons. Of all the widows in our sample 28 per cent were members of one of the traditional religions! Moreover, except for Christians, where the proportion is far greater than for the nonreligious category, single persons are considerably underrepresented in the religious groups.

The educational achievement of religious persons seems somewhat lower than it does for nonreligious persons, though this statement hides great differences among the religious groups. Eighty-eight per cent of the Christians are in the high educational level (indeed, 21 per cent of the Christians are college graduates, a far higher percentage than for any other group), but only one third of the members of the new religions were at the high education level. Sōka Gakkai members and adherents of the traditional religions were about equal in their educational attainment, both groups being well below the standard of nonreligious persons.

There were no great differences between all religious and all nonreligious persons concerning family average monthly income. But this statement too is quite misleading because of the great religious group differences. Sōka Gakkai members had by far the lowest average income, while Christians and members of the traditional religions were considerably above the average. Thirty-seven per cent of our Christian respondents had an average family monthly income of more than 100,000 yen.

Similar differences were found concerning occupation. Between religious and nonreligious persons generally there were no differences, but between the groups themselves, the variations were quite large. Sōka Gakkai members were overwhelmingly shop workers and laborers, while Christians and adherents of the new religions were predominantly in the professional, managerial, white collar class (although the table does not show it, more students were Christians than were found in any other religious category).

Finally, while there were no great differences between religious and nonreligious persons generally concerning interviewer-determined social class for our Tokyo respondents, there were considerable differences between the religious groups. Christians had the highest class status of all and Sōka Gakkai members by far the lowest.

In summary, then, religious persons as a whole were different from nonreligious persons in being predominantly women, older, of lower education, and having fewer single and more widowed persons. On income, occupation, class, and proportion of married persons, there were no differences.

On most measures, however, there were differences between each of the religious groups themselves and persons of no religion which were substantially greater than the differences simply between religious and nonreligious persons. Members of the traditional religions were much older, somewhat less well educated, more likely to have been widowed and to have a higher income. Members of the new religions were predominantly women, older, less likely to be single, much less well educated, and of slightly higher occupational status. Sōka Gakkai members were less well educated and of far lower income, occupational status, and social class. Finally, Christians were overwhelmingly females, young, highly educated, rich, and of high occupational and social class.

We shall see how these various groups differ in social attitudes later.

4. *Leader-follower differences.* It may be recalled that Suzuki's study was of Sōka Gakkai members alone. As part of his analysis he divided his respondents into leaders and followers on the basis of their rank and position in the Sōka Gakkai. As we saw before, the Sōka Gakkai has a great number of achieved status positions, such as *kumi-chō* and *han-chō* for men, and *kumi-tan* and *han-tan* for women. There are also block leaders, youth division leaders, and the like, as well as the teaching ranks. The achievement of any of these positions seemed to designate a member as a leader for Suzuki's purposes, while ordinary members were classified as followers. Suzuki discovered many differences between the two groups on the basis of their evaluation of the teachings and activities of

the Sōka Gakkai, but we are here interested in the demographic differences he found.

Briefly, 40 per cent of Suzuki's leaders had incomes of 30,000 yen or more, and only 17 per cent had incomes of 15,000 yen or less, while the corresponding figures for the followers were 29 and 33 per cent. Similarly, while the educational attainment of 56 per cent of the leaders was middle school or less, and 14 per cent had a college education, 65 per cent of the followers had fulfilled only the basic educational requirements, while but 7 per cent had gone to college. As far as their fathers' occupations were concerned, both the leaders and the followers were overwhelmingly from agricultural and small shop families, but twice as many leaders as followers came from service occupations. In regard to their own occupations, the leaders were mainly small, private, commercial enterprisers, while the followers were predominantly shop clerks or manual laborers.[14]

In short, while the Sōka Gakkai members in Fukuoka as a whole were of lower status, according to income, education, and occupation, the followers were far lower than the leaders.

5. *When the members joined.* We saw above that while according to official Sōka Gakkai membership figures, only about one third of the current members had joined during the seven years of Josei Toda's presidency (1951–58), two thirds of the Japanese testimonials in the *Seikyō Graphic* came from persons who had entered the Sōka Gakkai during that period. Suzuki, whose study ended in 1962, reported that 57 per cent of his respondents had joined in the seven years before 1960, while 43 per cent had joined in the first three years of Daisaku Ikeda's presidency. In our study, 56 per cent had become members during Ikeda's term and 44 per cent during Toda's. Thus, just as we concluded that the Japanese *Seikyō Graphic* testimonials came from members of long standing while the American testimonials in the *Seikyo News* were from recent converts, so we must also say that the persons in the *Seikyō Graphic* are members of more experience in the organization than the ordinary member.

6. *Reasons for joining.* It will also be recollected that both

[14] Suzuki, "Toshi Kasō no Shūkyō Shūdan," pp. 86–89.

the American and Japanese testimonials were full of accounts of distresses which the Sōka Gakkai members had before joining the Sōka Gakkai, and how they were subsequently relieved. We specifically asked our Sōka Gakkai respondents whether or not they had had any particular troubles before joining the Sōka Gakkai, and 36 per cent frankly said they had not. However, of the remaining, 25 per cent each mentioned a financial or health problem, 5 per cent said they had a problem of human relations, and 9 per cent did not specify the nature of their complaint.

Hayasaka also found that nearly 60 per cent of the Sōka Gakkai members gave "negative" reasons for joining the Sōka Gakkai, such as poor health (26 per cent), economic distresses (3 per cent), poor human relations (7 per cent), and various other troubles (23 per cent). Twenty-three per cent of his respondents also gave a "positive" reason for joining, such as the spiritual and psychological benefits they expected to receive from membership in the Sōka Gakkai, while 19 per cent gave "neutral" reasons, such as the fact that others in their family were already members.[15]

A somewhat different pattern was found in the Tokyo Universities' study in that 43 per cent cited a problem of human relations, and only 4 per cent an economic difficulty, while 26 per cent gave sickness as the reason and 8 per cent some other distress; 18 per cent also said they joined because others in their family were members.[16]

Thus, while the distribution of specific distresses among the three samples varies somewhat, still we do notice that roughly 60 per cent of the members said the reason they joined the Sōka Gakkai was to gain relief from some psychological, mental, or economic distress, while about 20 per cent of the members joined "naturally": that is, they became members because this was the religion of their family.

This last statement is a finding of some importance. The reputation of the Sōka Gakkai has been almost entirely bad. The forceful conversion techniques of *shakubuku* have been

---

[15] Hayasaka, *Shinkō Shūkyō*, p. 59. The terms "negative," "positive," and "neutral," were used by Hayasaka.

[16] Tokyo Universities, *Sōka Gakkai*, p. 59.

severely condemned. Moreover, many people complained about Sōka Gakkai members who chanted the Daimoku late at night, on crowded trains, or the like. The Sōka Gakkai had several brushes with the law, too, especially during election time when it was not always clear whether the members were attempting to convert to their religion or engaging in door-to-door campaigns for Sōka Gakkai election candidates, such campaigning methods being illegal under Japan's election laws.[17]

Even today the Sōka Gakkai is far from enjoying a good reputation among the Japanese people. Of the 1,500 persons questioned by NTV Television in their telepoll in the spring of 1964, 42 per cent chose the word "fanatical" to describe the Sōka Gakkai, and only 2 per cent of the persons interviewed said they would consider voting for the Kōseiren (the Clean Government Council, at that time a branch of the Sōka Gakkai, now formally separate and renamed Kōmeitō, the Clean Government Party).

Hayasaka applied a form of the semantic differential to his respondents, asking the non-Sōka Gakkai members to evaluate the term "Sōka Gakkai members" and the Sōka Gakkai members to evaluate the term "non-Sōka Gakkai members." According to his data, nonmembers considered Sōka Gakkai members to be very "active," "positive," and "loud," relatively "hard" and "restrained," and neutral regarding the "bright-dark," "young-old," and "dominant-submissive" dichotomies.

[17] For example, according to newspaper accounts, the Osaka District Court found several Sōka Gakkai members guilty of violating the election laws during the House of Councillors election of 1956 (*Japan Times*, March 7, 1961). Twenty Sōka Gakkai members were fined for a similar violation during the 1959 campaign (*Japan Times*, June 25, 1962). After three Sōka Gakkai members had been acquitted by the Tōkyō District Court in 1963, the Tokyo High Court fined them 15,000 yen each for obstructing the 1962 House of Councillors campaign (*Japan Times*, March 12, 1964). Finally, according to the *Japan Times* of April 30, 1964, the Election Law Amendment Special Committee of the House of Representatives studied the matter regarding "a certain religious organization which is applying certain campaign tactics to change the legal addresses of a vast number of its followers to a certain area in order to win the election." The Sōka Gakkai has been accused of resorting to such techniques.

On the other hand, Sōka Gakkai members considered non-members to be very "passive," "old," and "negative," moderately "dark," "hard," "restrained," and "loud," and neutral concerning dominance-submissiveness.[18]

We asked our non–Sōka Gakkai respondents four different questions about their attitudes toward the Sōka Gakkai and its activities. On all four items, the number of respondents positively oriented toward the Sōka Gakkai was small indeed.

a. *What do you think of the Sōka Gakkai?* Only 4 per cent of the non–Sōka Gakkai respondents said that they liked the Sōka Gakkai, while 57 per cent disliked it; 16 per cent gave neutral answers, and 23 per cent declined to answer the question.

b. *Have you ever considered joining the Sōka Gakkai?* Again, only 4 per cent of our respondents who were not already members of the Sōka Gakkai said they had thought of joining it, and 5 per cent would not say whether they had or not. Ninety-one per cent replied that they never had considered joining. Of these, 41 per cent said either that they were not interested in it or any other religion, or that they had a religion of their own. However, 44 per cent—more than in any other category—volunteered the statement that they disliked the Sōka Gakkai and would never join it.

c. *Some people say the Sōka Gakkai is bad for the Japanese people, some say it is not. What do you think?* Even though most of our respondents were reluctant to state that the Sōka Gakkai was positively bad for Japan, 30 per cent of them frankly did say so. A high of 38 per cent of the non–Sōka Gakkai people we interviewed refused to commit themselves one way or the other on this question, and 32 per cent declared that the Sōka Gakkai was not necessarily bad for Japan, most of them stating that the Sōka Gakkai had its good points, too, and that anyway, the principle of freedom of religion must be observed.

d. *What do you think of the political activities of the Sōka Gakkai?* Here again, only 4 per cent of the non–Sōka Gakkai members said that they approved of the political activities of

[18] Hayasaka, *Shinkō Shūkyō*, pp. 36–37.

the Sōka Gakkai, while 58 per cent disapproved; 12 per cent took a neutral position, and 26 per cent said they did not know.

Thus we can conclude that our respondents generally were quite negatively oriented toward the Sōka Gakkai. Yet, even though their number is small, we were interested in finding out what groups of people were favorably disposed toward the Sōka Gakkai, because it is probably from them that the Sōka Gakkai gains its new members.

Interestingly, we discovered that on questions *a, c,* and *d,* above, there were no demographic pattern differences which would distinguish the few who liked the Sōka Gakkai from the many who did not. Whether we compared by religious affiliation, political party, education, sex, occupation, income, age, marital status, or belief in God, those who liked the Sōka Gakkai were not significantly different from those who disliked it.

Concerning question *b,* however, there was a slight, though statistically insignificant, difference which we report in order to suggest what actually may be an important fact: although there was no difference between those who had considered joining the Sōka Gakkai and those who had not on the basis of religious affiliation, sex, or age, we did find that persons of lower social status were slightly more likely to report that they had considered joining the Sōka Gakkai than were persons of higher social status. Of persons in shop and labor occupations 6 per cent said they had considered joining, while only 2 per cent of those in professional, managerial, or white collar professions said they had; 7 per cent of those with income below 40,000 yen per month said they had considered joining the Sōka Gakkai compared to only 3 per cent of those with incomes above 40,000 yen; 6 per cent of the single persons said that they had, to 3 per cent of the married persons; 6 per cent of the Socialist and of the Democratic Socialist party members and also 6 per cent of those with no party affiliation said that they had considered joining, but only 2 per cent of the Liberal Democratic affiliates said that they had.

Most interesting, 25 per cent of our respondents who said that they did not know whether they believed in God or not,

11 per cent of those who had once believed in God but did not now, 5 per cent of those who said they *did* believe in God, but only 2 per cent of those who said they definitely did not, declared that they had considered joining the Sōka Gakkai.

Finally, as on other occasions, level of education seemed to be lineally related to willingness to join the Sōka Gakkai: 7 per cent of those with only an elementary school education, 6 per cent of those with a middle school education, 4 per cent of those who had gone to high school, and only 1 per cent of persons who had been to college said that they had considered joining the Sōka Gakkai.

Thus we conclude that as far as our sample of Tokyo residents is concerned, there is no difference between the demographic groups as far as dislike toward the Sōka Gakkai is concerned. However, lower-status persons and those uncertain about the existence of God are slightly more likely to have considered joining the Sōka Gakkai than are higher-status persons or people sure either that God does exist or that he does not. There is no demographic group in our sample, however, that can be said to be decidedly disposed toward joining the Sōka Gakkai, and among all groups the Sōka Gakkai is strongly disliked.

There are some signs that the Sōka Gakkai is domesticating. Since 1964, for example, the Sōka Gakkai media have been urging members to be more "socially responsible people" (*shakai-teki ningen*). It has specifically enjoined the members not to disturb others by chanting the Daimoku at inconvenient hours or in inconvenient places. It also has encouraged the use of *shōju*, a milder method of conversion than *shakubuku*.[19]

This change may be due partly to the rising self-confidence of the Sōka Gakkai and to their realization of their unnecessarily negative—and hence conversion-inhibiting—reputation. On the other hand, and this is where it ties in with our data on why people joined the Sōka Gakkai, it may in part be

[19] Most of the *Seikyō Graphic* for August 13, 1964, was devoted to improving the members' *shakaisei* (social consciousness). Included were a number of interesting cartoons, especially on pp. 10–11, showing believers disturbing others by praying loudly at night, chanting the Daimoku in front of stores (like beggar-monks), or neglecting their children and businesses in order to pray.

the result of the rise of the number of "natural" second-genera-tion members in its midst, whose loyalty to and dependence on the Sōka Gakkai may be no less intense than that of those who were first converted, but who may be less willing to use tech-niques of conversion which are as thoroughly "un-Japanese" as *shakubuku*. Indeed, on the basis of this admittedly fragmentary evidence, we can expect the Sōka Gakkai to follow the typical road of "evangelical" religious organizations, and gradually soften its attacks on other religions and nonbelievers, increase its appeal to and proportion of membership among the upper-middle classes, and hence eventually alienate itself from the lower classes who were its first converts—necessitating, no doubt, another "reformation" in the future in order to serve the needs of the lower strata of Japanese society.

Additional Demographic and Attitudinal Comparisons

In attempting to determine in what other ways Sōka Gakkai members were different from nonmembers, we included a num-ber of additional demographic items in our survey that we hypothesized would be significant.

1. *Marital status.* The other surveys cited above did not give data on the marital status of Sōka Gakkai members, and the available evidence, closely related to postulated age and sex differences, did not enable us to predict what the situation would be. Some reports stated that the Sōka Gakkai is com-posed mostly of young unmarried men and older women. But the Sōka Gakkai itself strongly stresses total family conversion. In our survey, as we saw above, somewhat more of the Sōka Gakkai members were married, widowed, or divorced than was the total sample, and there were fewer single members, but these differences were not statistically significant, so we cannot conclude that Sōka Gakkai members in Tokyo are different on this indicator from the population generally.[20]

2. *Health.* We have repeatedly seen that Sōka Gakkai testi-monials and survey data show that many members say that they joined to gain relief from some illness. This was true

[20] There was no difference even when we controlled for sex and age.

in our sample as well. But when we asked all of our respondents whether they had, in the past year, suffered from some illness that had interfered with their work or normal daily routine, no more than 6 per cent either of the total sample or of the Sōka Gakkai subsample replied that they had. It will be recalled that 25 per cent of the Sōka Gakkai members in our survey gave a reason pertaining to sickness as their motivation for joining. Does this indicate that Sōka Gakkai members have returned to normal health? We do not believe the questions leading up to the one concerning sickness should have encouraged the respondents to "forget" their illnesses, nor do we see why the respondents should otherwise have misrepresented the situation. Perhaps some Sōka Gakkai members responded stereotypically concerning their reasons for joining the Sōka Gakkai, or perhaps they were, as we have seen in the testimonials, speaking of a sickness of someone else in their family, not themselves. In any event, we do not have evidence that Sōka Gakkai members are any more or less healthy than the general Tokyo population.

The brand research study, however, did reveal that of 29 types of patent medicine, *Seikyō Shimbun* subscribers bought an average of 11.5 per cent *less* on 18 types than did the non–Sōka Gakkai sample, the same on 10 types, and 8 per cent more on only one (prickly heat powder). Yet Sōka Gakkai members used an average of 9 per cent *more* cosmetics and soap than did nonmembers on 13 items, the same on 13, and 7 per cent less on only 1 (men's cosmetic cream).[21]

3. *Human relations.* We also saw that many Sōka Gakkai members stated in their testimonials that they had problems of human relations, frequently quarreling with their friends or family, being shy and timid, and having few friends. We included questions tapping this dimension in our Tokyo survey as well. We asked our respondents whether they would say they had many friends, few friends, or almost no friends. Whereas only 12 per cent of the total sample said they had almost no friends, 22 per cent of the Sōka Gakkai sample so replied. We further asked our married respondents to evaluate the understanding they were getting from their husband or wife.

[21] *Seikyō Brand Research*, pp. 12–13.

While 35 per cent of the total population said it was good or excellent, only 28 per cent of the Sōka Gakkai members chose this response.

Both these indicators, pertaining to relations with friends and family, show Sōka Gakkai members on the more "undesirable" range of responses. But because of the size of our Sōka Gakkai subsample, neither response is statistically significant.

4. *Satisfaction with life.* We do have evidence, significant at the .001 level, which indicates that our Sōka Gakkai members are far less satisfied with life generally than was the total sample. We asked our respondents to tell us whether they were satisfied with their present life or not. Only 23 per cent of the total sample said they were not, compared to 47 per cent of the Sōka Gakkai members. While satisfaction with life also correlates with income (29 per cent of those whose families have less than the average monthly wage of 59,000 yen are dissatisfied, while only 16 per cent of those above this average are discontented), the evidence here indicates that membership in the Sōka Gakkai does not make people feel more contented with their lives.

5. *Attitudes toward work.* Elsewhere we have reported on the existence of an analogue to the Protestant Ethic in Japanese society which would help account for Japan's phenomenal economic growth.[22] A question used as one of the indicators of this analogue queried what type of person our respondents would like to be: a hard worker, friendly, a person who could do things better than others, one who is lucky, or one who has no worries.[23] Of the non–Sōka Gakkai members, 79 per cent chose either "a hard worker," "a person who has no worries," or "a person who is friendly." But only 54 per cent of the Sōka Gakkai members chose one of these three. Instead, 46 per cent of the Sōka Gakkai sample chose either "a person who can do things better than others" or "a person who is lucky," a combination chosen by only 21 per cent of the non–Sōka Gakkai sample. This difference is significant at .001.

[22] James Allen Dator, "The 'Protestant Ethic' in Japan," *Journal of Developing Areas*, I (October, 1966), 23–40.
[23] The questions were derived from Gerhard Lenski, *The Religious Factor* (Garden City, N.Y.: Doubleday, 1961), Appendix.

We have discussed more fully the implications of this in the article cited above. Briefly, this and other items indicate the existence of a positive attitude toward the value of hard work on the part of the Tokyo (and, by other data, Japanese) citizens, coupled with a minimum of personal "drive" or "big plans," and a desire to get along well with others. This was especially true for the middle and lower classes. Generally, only the professional classes and those with a college education indicated a desire to be able to do things better than others. Thus there appears to be in Japan a large mass of hard-working and diligent, if unimaginative, people, who are led by a well-educated and adventuresome entrepreneurial elite.

The Sōka Gakkai members presented the major exception to this generalization. According to their educational and occupational standards, they should have been even less ambitious than the average, but, to the contrary, they had the highest "do things better" response of any subclassification. But they also had the highest "lucky" response and the lowest "hard worker." Thus, the evidence accords with the hypothesis that while Sōka Gakkai members are a very ambitious group, they are more willing to rely indirectly upon forces external to themselves (such as the Gohonzon?) in order to achieve their aims than to attack the problem directly by working hard.[24] In part this may be because their educational achievements are much lower than those of the general population, and in Japan, educational achievement, rather than subsequent hard work, tends to determine worldly position and success. On the other hand, because educational attainment itself depends largely upon a willingness to study diligently in order to pass the many difficult examinations that provide access to the better academic institutions, it is not unreasonable to suggest that perhaps the Sōka Gakkai members lacked the self-discipline and/or ability necessary to get the required education in the first place.

Another item in the "Protestant Ethic" series asked our respondents what they would prefer in a job: high income, no

---

[24] In this regard, it is interesting to find that while 80 per cent of all Tokyo citizens have life insurance policies, only 50 per cent of the *Seikyō Shimbun* subscribers do. *Seikyō Brand Research*, p. 82.

chance of being fired, lots of free time, chances for advancement, or important work. Here also, the Sōka Gakkai subsample differed significantly from the average. While the highest single choice of all respondents was "important work" (45 per cent), only 36 per cent of the Sōka Gakkai subsample chose this, and 40 per cent elected "high income," which was chosen by only 28 per cent of the total sample. This distribution was unaffected when income was controlled.

6. *Previous religious affiliation.* It will be recalled that only sixteen of our two hundred *Seikyō Graphic* testimonials mentioned what religion they had previously been affiliated with. We suggested that this might indicate that most of them had not been members of any religion before joining the Sōka Gakkai because this is true of approximately 75 per cent of the Japanese population. Our survey data indicated that this was probably the case, because 78 per cent of our respondents said they were members of no religion before joining the Sōka Gakkai. The remaining replies were sprinkled throughout the great variety of religious groups in Japan and did not indicate they came predominantly from any one religious group.

Most Japanese, however, recognize that their family traditionally was affiliated with some religious group, and we asked our respondents to tell us what that was. Of our total sample, 12 per cent said their family had no religious affiliation, and 20 per cent said they did not know. Of the remaining, 2 per cent said Shintō, 10 per cent Nichiren Shū (not the sect with which Sōka Gakkai is affiliated), 62 per cent gave some other Buddhist sect, 1.3 per cent Christian, 0.6 per cent the Sōka Gakkai (all but two of these respondents were themselves Sōka Gakkai members), and 0.7 per cent some other religious group. Except for the fact that 9 per cent of our Sōka Gakkai members said their traditional family religion was Nichiren Shōshū (i.e., Sōka Gakkai), the responses were not significantly different for Sōka Gakkai members alone. The same is true when we asked them what the religion of their family and their mother was.

There was a difference concerning the religion of their spouse, because 59 per cent of the married Sōka Gakkai members indicated that their husband or wife was in the Sōka

Gakkai. In fact, only seven of the nonmembers reported having a Sōka Gakkai spouse. However, this is not significantly different from any other religious group, or for those with no religion: if the respondent had any religious affiliation at all—or if he had none—it was generally the same as that of his spouse.

Thus we do not find from our evidence that Sōka Gakkai members are drawn from any particular former religious group. But other studies of religious behavior[25] have indicated that religious converts generally are persons who come from "religious families." That is, people who are members of religious groups are more likely to have been reared in families which accepted some religious faith than are persons who have no religious affiliation.

What was the situation for our Sōka Gakkai respondents? If we ignore the *particular* religious denomination and simply see whether or not their parents were members of *any* religious group, did our Sōka Gakkai respondents tend to come from "religious homes"? If so, were they more likely or less likely to have come from religious homes than were members of other religions?

As we saw above, in our questionnaire we had three measures of the religious affiliation of our respondents' parents: their family's traditional religion, their father's religion, and their mother's religion. The differences in the patterns of responses between these three indicators, and among the different religious groups, is quite interesting.

First, if we compare the responses of all persons who had any religious affiliation with those who had none, we find support for the thesis that religious adults generally come from religious homes: 85 per cent of the 171 persons in our survey who were members of some religious group were able to identify their family's traditional religion, 8 per cent said their family had no traditional religion, and 7 per cent were unable to recall whether they had one or not; but only 75 per cent of the 803 persons who had no religion identified their family's

---

[25] Michael Argyle, *Religious Behaviour* (London: Routledge & Kegan Paul, 1958), pp. 39–42, and Walter H. Clark, *The Oxford Group* (New York: Bookman Associates, 1951), p. 228.

religion, 13 per cent said they had none, and 12 per cent did not know (significant at >.01).

Second, as far as their mother's religion was concerned, while only 24 per cent of those with no religion said their mothers had some religious affiliation and 70 per cent said they did not, 48 per cent of the members with any religion said their mothers also were religious affiliates and 46 per cent said they were not (significant at >.001).

Finally, only 19 per cent of our respondents with no religion said their fathers had a religious faith, and 74 per cent said they had none, while 42 per cent of those with a religion said their fathers also had a religion and 54 per cent said they did not (significant at >.001).

Thus we can conclude that religious persons do tend to come from religious families. But when we see what the situation is for *specific* religious groups, we find that Sōka Gakkai members are *not* more likely to have come from religious families by any of the three indicators used than are persons with no religious affiliation: 80 per cent of the Sōka Gakkai members identified their family religion, 35 per cent said their mother had a religion, and 20 per cent said their father was a member of some religion. Inspection shows that this distribution is not significantly different from that of respondents with no religion.

The situation was quite different, however, for the members of the traditional Japanese religions (Shintō and all Buddhist groups): 97 per cent of them revealed that their family had a traditional religion, 65 per cent said their mother had a religion, and 57 per cent said their father had a religion.

For Christians and for members of the other newer religions (Tenrikyō, Risshō Kōsei Kai, and so forth) the results were mixed: while only 56 per cent of the members of the newer religions identified their family religion (the lowest of any religious group, and even significantly lower than for non-affiliates) 50 per cent said their mother had a religion and 44 per cent said their father had one. Christians, on the other hand, ranked exactly as high as the traditional religious affiliates on family religion: 97 per cent identified their family religion, but only 31 per cent (the lowest of any religious group, and about equal to that of persons with no religion) named their mother's religion, while 41 per cent (about average for religious affiliates) named their father's religion.

Thus, while there is an indication that persons of any religious affiliation are more likely than persons of no religion to come from religious families, it is only for members of the traditional religions, and definitely not for Sōka Gakkai members, that we find evidence that this is the case for specific religions. The situation for Christians and members of the newer religions is mixed.

Related to this question of the influence of family religiosity upon personal religious affiliation is another question we included in our survey. We handed all of our respondents a card and asked them which items written on it had most influenced their religious beliefs. The replies were quite varied.

First, although 25 per cent of the persons with any religion said it was their parents that most influenced their religious beliefs, and only 18 per cent of the persons with no religion chose this response, and while 32 per cent of those with no religion said nothing had influenced them and only 5 per cent of the religious affiliates made this choice, the replies of the religious and nonreligious respondents (except for the "nothing" category) were not significantly different.

Among the various religious groups, however, there were interesting differences: 45 per cent (more than any other group) of the adherents of the traditional religions said that their parents had most influenced their religious beliefs, while only 13 per cent of the Sōka Gakkai members made this response, 27 per cent of them indicating their spouses or children, and 33 per cent their friends (only 10 per cent each of the traditional affiliates chose these alternatives) as those who had most influenced them. Christians mostly (41 per cent) indicated either a priest or a teacher, a choice made by only 11 per cent of the traditional members and 4 per cent of the Sōka Gakkai members. The replies of the members of the newer religions were spread nearly equally among all the choices presented to them.

Hence we conclude (and this conclusion is supported by information found elsewhere in this report) that the religious beliefs of Sōka Gakkai members are most influenced by their spouses, children, or friends, while Christians indicated priests or teachers, and traditional adherents their parents.

Relating this to the questions asked several paragraphs above, we can conclude that it is only for the members of traditional religions in Japan that we can agree that coming from a religious family is likely to influence adult religious affiliation positively, and that personal contact and intergroup life are more likely to be determinant for membership in one of the newer religious expressions in Japan, here including Christians and Sōka Gakkai members.

7. *Residence mobility.* It has been said that the Sōka Gakkai, which is generally stronger in urban than in rural areas, appeals especially to persons who have only recently come to the large and impersonal cities from tightly knit rural communities. This thesis is surely plausible enough, but, unfortunately, we did not get enough evidence from our Tokyo study either to confirm or deny this theory definitely.

The very first question we asked our respondents was how long they had lived at their present address. Thirty-seven per cent replied either that they had always lived there or had spent half or more of their lives at their present address; 30 per cent said they had lived there from 5 to 10 years; and 33 per cent indicated less than 5 years. Of the Sōka Gakkai members, however, 45 per cent indicated that they were indeed recent arrivals, replying that they had lived at their present address for less than 5 years. This was a shorter time than was the case for any other religious category, though it was approximated by Christians, 40 per cent of whom said they had recently moved to their present address. Indeed, only 19 per cent of the Christians said they had lived at their present address all or over one half of their lives.

The situation was quite different for members of the "traditional" Japanese religions (Shintō and all Buddhist groups): 60 per cent said they had spent more than half their lives at the present address, while only 18 per cent had arrived in the past 5 years. Members of the other new religions (Tenrikyō, Risshō Kōsei Kai, etc.) also were older residents than were either Christian or Sōka Gakkai members: 18 per cent had arrived less than 5 years before, and 40 per cent had spent more than half their lives at their present address.

Thus, if we were to rank our respondents by their religious affiliation according to their length of residence at the address where we interviewed them, we would find that the ranking would be, from longest to shortest period of residence: traditional religions and new religions at one end, no religious affiliation in the middle, and Christians and Sōka Gakkai members at the other extreme.

When, however, we asked our respondents who had spent less than all of their lives at the present address where they had lived previously, we could find no indication at all that they had moved from a rural location to Tokyo: between 73 and 79 per cent of all religious groups, including the Sōka Gakkai, had lived in another section of Tokyo, 11 per cent said they had lived near Tokyo, 4 per cent said they had moved to Tokyo from some other urban area, and only 12 per cent said they had lived in a rural area. The Sōka Gakkai respondents did not differ significantly from these over-all totals. Indeed, only the replies from Christians were markedly at odds with this pattern, for not a single Christian said he had moved to Tokyo from a rural area.

Hence, while we may conclude from this admittedly imperfect evidence that Sōka Gakkai members are more recent arrivals at their present addresses, and seem to be decidedly more mobile than members of either the traditional or newer religions, our Sōka Gakkai respondents seemed not to come from rural areas much more than did the average respondent.

We conclude, then, that the Sōka Gakkai members are in the lower, but not lowest, socioeconomic strata of Japanese society; that they are a somewhat less satisfied and more "friendless" group; that they generally had no religious affiliation before joining the Sōka Gakkai, and joined to relieve a physical, mental, or sociological distress, although about one fifth joined because others in their family were members before them. We saw that Sōka Gakkai members had attitudes toward work that seemed to be quite atypical of Japanese generally: they were less committed to hard work as a means of achieving their ends, and relied more on "luck."

In what other ways are the attitudes of Sōka Gakkai members similar to or different from those of the population generally? This is the topic of our next section on the personality of Japanese Sōka Gakkai members.

Personality of Japanese Members

It is not our purpose here to examine all aspects of the personality of Japanese Sōka Gakkai members. Rather, we will try to discover which of two extant hypotheses about Sōka Gakkai members is correct.

A frequent claim by the critics of the Sōka Gakkai is that Sōka Gakkai members are more authoritarian, alienated, and undemocratic than are nonmembers. Thus, Sōka Gakkai members could be expected to rank lower (i.e., at the "undesirable" ends) on personality scales than would the population from which they were drawn. Thus we would expect scale scores to show that Sōka Gakkai members are more authoritarian, more submissive, more anomic, more cabalistic, less euphoric, have less faith in people, and so forth, than a sample of non–Sōka Gakkai Japanese.

An alternate hypothesis, also possible, is that the Sōka Gakkai "cures" the personality "defects" of persons who are attracted to it. Sōka Gakkai members may score higher ("better") than the average on personality scales because of the therapeutic effect of Sōka Gakkai membership. This is the claim of the Sōka Gakkai itself.

Which hypothesis is correct? We have two comparative studies of Sōka Gakkai and non–Sōka Gakkai members which will help us explore this problem. One is our own study of Tokyo. The other is the research by Hayasaka that we have utilized before in the demographic section. Let us turn to the Hayasaka study once again.

1. *Hayasaka's findings.* Hayasaka included in his study a battery of forty items, in the usual five-point agree-disagree format, intending to construct a scale to measure tradition-directed attitudes (*Dentō-teki shikō taidō*). After analysis by a split halves method, ten of the items were discarded, and the

remaining thirty were clustered into seven subcategories of traditionalism, entitled "Superior-Inferior Relations," "Familism," "Filial Piety," "Main Family–Branch Family Relations," "Hometown Consciousness," "Desire for Harmony," and "Conventional Conduct." [26]

The results showed that the total sample might be considered slightly tradition-directed on the over-all scale, but when the seven component subscales were examined, the observed mean did not significantly differ from the theoretical mean on any but the "Familism" and the "Conventional Behavior" subscales, where the results showed measurable traditionalism. The replies for the total sample were also cross tabulated by sex, age, education, personal monthly income, and occupation. No difference was found according to sex, income, or occupation, but there was a significant and continuous difference by age. That is, the youngest age group (20–29) was judged to be "rather non-tradition-directed," while those in the oldest group (50 and over) were "very tradition-directed." Respondents in their thirties were "somewhat non-tradition-directed," and those in their forties "somewhat tradition-directed." Concerning education also, there were some differences: those with elementary or middle school education being more tradition-directed than those with a college education, while high school educated respondents were in the middle. But the difference between the education extremes was not as great as the difference between the age groups.

Like ourselves, Hayasaka was primarily interested in discovering if there were differences between Sōka Gakkai and non–Sōka Gakkai members. A comparison of all Sōka Gakkai members with all nonmembers on the total scale and on each of the seven subcategories failed to reveal any differences at all; the mean score of both groups clustered tightly around the theoretical mean. Cross tabulation by demographic categories was illuminating, however. Except for sex, which showed no difference between the two groups, the replies of Sōka Gakkai members in the other categories were considerably less widely spread than were those of the nonmembers. That is, the replies of the Sōka Gakkai members to the total scale and to all

[26] A translation of the thirty items of the scale is given in Appendix II.

TABLE 10

SIX PERSONALITY SCALES' PERCENTAGE OF "UNDESIRABLE" RESPONSES
BY SIX RELIGIOUS CATEGORIES OF THE 1965 TOKYO SAMPLE

		(N)
Alienation (High)		
No religion	30	(793)
All religions	34	(171)
Traditional religions	34	(62)
New religions	50	(32)
Sōka Gakkai	38	(45)
Christians	16	(32)
(N)	(296)	(964)
Authoritarianism (High)		
No religion	35	(793)
All religions	41	(168)
Traditional religions	45	(60)
New religions	37	(31)
Sōka Gakkai	42	(45)
Christians	12	(32)
(N)	(351)	(961)
Anomie (High)		
No religion	19	(793)
All religions	25	(172)
Traditional religions	27	(63)
New religions	37	(32)
Sōka Gakkai	24	(45)
Christians	9	(32)
(N)	(197)	(965)
Faith in People (Low)		
No religion	39	(797)
All religions	40	(171)
Traditional religions	44	(62)
New religions	32	(32)
Sōka Gakkai	56	(45)
Christians	19	(32)
(N)	(379)	(968)
Mistrust of Public Officials (High)		
No religion	70	(752)
All religions	65	(160)
Traditional religions	64	(57)
New religions	68	(29)
Sōka Gakkai	64	(42)
Christians	64	(32)
(N)	(631)	(912)

Citizen Duty (Low)		
No religion	12	(792)
All religions	16	(171)
Traditional religions	17	(63)
New religions	25	(32)
Sōka Gakkai	9	(44)
Christians	9	(32)
(N)	(121)	(963)

(N) = number of cases on which percentages are based.

of its seven subcategories were more homogeneous than were the replies of the nonmembers. Moreover, as we saw before, since the attitudes of all Sōka Gakkai members tended to be neutral on this measure, Sōka Gakkai members can be considered neither particularly tradition-directed nor opposed to traditional values. Thus the differences between the extremes of age and education, noted for the total sample, are actually somewhat increased for nonmembers, but considerably reduced for Sōka Gakkai members when the two groups are analyzed separately.

Hayasaka suggests this homogeneity of attitudes for Sōka Gakkai members is a function of that organization's *hanashi-ai* (small group discussions). Thus, while Hayasaka's scale measured tradition-directed orientation and not social alienation, it is of importance to us in indicating that while the attitudes of Sōka Gakkai members, in comparison with nonmembers, are neither more strongly in support of, nor opposed to, traditional Japanese social relations, the attitudes of Sōka Gakkai members are more homogeneous than those of nonmembers. But this is probably true of most viable voluntary organizations, and is not by itself a finding of great assistance to us here.

2. *Our findings.* Hayasaka's scales were plainly designed for Japanese subjects only. Partly to provide a different dimension of analysis, and partly to facilitate cross-cultural comparisons, we adopted five scales that have been widely used in the United States.[27]

Table 10 gives the results for all five of these scales, and for

[27] All of the cross-cultural comparisons, however, will not be presented in this report. The five scales used were designed to measure authoritarianism, anomie, faith in people, mistrust of public officials, and a sense of citizen duty. The items composing each of these scales and the full references for them are in Appendix III.

the composite index of social alienation derived by the inclusion of all scale items into one inventory. We have displayed the data according to six religious affiliation categories. It will be recalled that more than 80 per cent of our Tokyo respondents said they belonged to no religious organization. Thus, there is very little difference between the replies of those who were members of no religious organization and those of the total population. Hence, total population responses are not given in this table.

There are significant differences according to the religious categories, however. First, though comprising only 3.3 per cent of the total sample (but 19 per cent of those with any religion), Christians are shown to be almost uniformly on the "desirable" end of all the scales. ("Desirable" here means disagreement with items indicating authoritarianism, anomie, and mistrust of public officials, and agreement with items showing faith in people and a sense of citizen duty.) Members of all other religions (i.e., excepting Sōka Gakkai adherents and Christians) scored more often in the "undesirable" direction. The replies of Sōka Gakkai members were most often nearly the same as those of the total sample, save for an indication of considerably less "faith in people" and for a slightly more "undesirable" score on the authoritarianism scale and the combined social aliena-tion scale. Before interpreting this, however, we should examine the pattern of responses of the total sample to the five separate scales and to the composite.

Broadly summarizing, it might seem that according to this measure of social alienation, the Tokyo population may be con-sidered nearly evenly split into three groups. Nearly an equal number scored "undesirable" as scored "desirable" and only slightly more were neutral. Yet this is merely an artifact of our scoring method which was designed to provide a cultural base by which to evaluate groups within the sample, rather than a statement of social alienation of Tokyo citizens as measured by some objective—or arbitrary—standard. This was not the case of the five separate scales, however, where we followed the scor-ing methods used in the original studies from which they were derived. Thus, it can be suggested that by these measures, Tōkyō citizens generally are somewhat authoritarian, have little faith in people, and considerable distrust of public officials, but that they are not anomic and have a very high sense of citizen duty. While questions can surely be raised about the cultural appropriateness of some individual items on the inventory, the general conclusion seems to be in accord with similar studies and with other reliable evaluations of modal Japanese personality.

It is tempting to discuss the implications of these various findings for Japanese society generally, but since our interest here is a comparison of Sōka Gakkai members with the population from which they were drawn, we shall restrict ourselves to commenting on this alone. As we see, Sōka Gakkai members appear generally not to be significantly different from the ordinary Tokyo citizen, but we will see there probably are differences indeed. Clearly they indicate far less faith in people than did even the general population, and the replies to some individual items on this scale were especially illuminating. On all five items, the Sōka Gakkai members were less trusting.[28] While 64 per cent of the nonreligious respondents agreed that "you can't be too careful in your dealings with people," 77 per cent of the Sōka Gakkai members did (>.10); 68 per cent of the nonreligious total agreed that "if you don't watch out, people will take advantage of you," compared to 89 per cent of the Sōka Gakkai members (>.05); 71 per cent of the total also said that "most people don't care about other people, but only look out for themselves," but this was the choice of 80 per cent of the members of the Sōka Gakkai (not statistically significant). On two items, the sample as a whole did indicate some faith in people. However, while 62 per cent of the respondents without a religion agreed that "most people are inclined to help others," only 51 per cent of the Sōka Gakkai members did (>.10); 75 per cent agreed that "most people can be trusted," but only 68 per cent of our Sōka Gakkai respondents agreed (not statistically significant).[29]

---

[28] It will be recalled that a significantly higher percentage of Sōka Gakkai members than nonmembers in our survey reported that they had "no friends." See pp. 85–86.

[29] It is interesting to compare these faith-in-people item responses with those that Almond and Verba obtained in their five-nation survey. See

Thus while the total sample was generally skeptical of other people, the Sōka Gakkai subsample was uniformly more so.[30] This might well be a reflection of the almost paranoiac attitude the Sōka Gakkai has toward nonmembers. We have seen that the Sōka Gakkai is almost universally condemned. Hayasaka's semantic differential data, cited above, showed that Sōka Gakkai members have a low evaluation of others. Moreover, the media

---

Gabriel Almond and Sydney Verba, *The Civic Culture* (Princeton, N.J.: Princeton University Press, 1963), p. 267:

	US (%)	UK (%)	Ger- many (%)	Italy (%)	Mexico (%)	Tokyo (%)	Soka Gakkai (%)	Chris- tian (%)
1 No one is going to care much what happens to you. . . .	38	45	72	61	78	. . .	. . .	. . .
2 If you don't watch out, people will take advantage of you.	68	75	81	73	94	68	88	66
3 Most people don't care about other people but only look out for themselves.	. . .	. . .	. . .	. . .	. . .	71	80	59
4 You can't be too careful in your dealings with people.	. . .	. . .	. . .	. . .	. . .	64	77	47
5 You can trust most people.	55	49	19	7	30	68	68	78
6 Most people are inclined to help others. . . .	31	28	15	5	15	62	51	63
7 Human nature is fundamentally cooperative.	80	84	58	55	82	. . .	. . .	. . .
(N)	(970)	(963)	(955)	(995)	(1,007)	(980)	(45)	(32)

We note several things from this. (1) At least on the faith-in-people dimension, our Tokyo respondents were *not* more misanthropic than the citizens of the five other countries. Indeed, on several, they ranked much "better" than even the American respondents who had been the "best" in Almond and Verba's study. (2) This was the only scale on which the Sōka Gakkai members were markedly "worse" than the average Tokyoite. (3) Christians were uniformly the most philanthropic of all.

[30] The Nagoya-area study, Tsuneo Muramatsu *et al.*, *Nihonjin* (Tōkyō: Reimei Shōbō, 1960), had two items which were similar to those on our faith-in-people scale. These were scored on a seven-point scale, four being the neutral position. The percentage of response was not reported. One item stated, "It is best to consider other people your enemies." The score to this—3.15—indicated considerable disagreement. However, another statement read, "You shouldn't speak to others without being careful of what you say." Here the score was 5.01. The responses of a sample of workers at about the same time also were in considerable agreement with this item. See James G. Abegglen, "Subordination and Autonomy Attitudes of Japanese Workers," *American Journal of Sociology*, LXIII (1957), 182.

of the Sōka Gakkai are strongly critical of anyone or any institution not affiliated with it. Journalists and scholars who have tried to interview leaders have also been struck by the at least defensive and often abusive nature of the encounter. As we have suggested, the Sōka Gakkai is making an effort to correct this overly critical tendency, but considerably more needs to be done. However, while the Sōka Gakkai itself is to blame in large measure for the negative evaluations others have of it, to a considerable extent the negative attitudes of the members themselves seem partly a defensive mechanism and partly a result of their own theological position which places the blame for all personal, social, and natural disorders on the shoulders of "false religion," that is, on all who are not believers in Nichiren Shōshū. It might well be, however, that this could be at least in some measure corrected if nonmembers—and especially the mass media—could be persuaded to take a more tolerant attitude toward the Sōka Gakkai.

While the Sōka Gakkai members are not significantly different from the average on any of the remaining four scales, on four of the individual items, Sōka Gakkai scores were lower, while on none did they score significantly higher:

1. In response to the statement, "the most important thing to teach children is absolute obedience to their parents," while only 30 per cent of the total sample agreed, 42 per cent of the Sōka Gakkai members did (>.10).

2. Of all respondents, 56 per cent agreed that "in spite of what some people say, the lot of the average man is getting worse, not better," but 75 per cent of the Sōka Gakkai members agreed that this was the case (>.02). This difference, of nineteen percentage points, was the greatest of any of the twenty-four items on the five scales.

3. Although the scores of the Sōka Gakkai members were close to the average on the "mistrust of public officials scale," on two of the four items which composed it, there were significant differences (>.10):

a. "Local officials soon lose touch with the people who elected them." Average agreement—68 per cent; Sōka Gakkai agreement —81 per cent.

b. "If people knew what was going on in high places, it would blow the lid off things." Average agreement—76 per cent; Sōka Gakkai agreement—88 per cent.

On four of the other fifteen items on the remaining scales (i.e., excluding "faith in people" and the above four items), Sōka Gakkai scores were lower, on another four they were higher, and on seven they were the same as the total sample scores. All of the differences were less than five percentage points, and none was statistically significant.

Just as in the case of Hayasaka's study, on none of the items or total scales were the Sōka Gakkai scores in the opposite direction from those of the total sample or of the nonmembers. That is, the modal personality of Sōka Gakkai members is not contrary to that of the ordinary Japanese. Rather, Sōka Gakkai members seem to emphasize more strongly the tendencies of the average: while all Tokyo citizens show little "faith in people," the Sōka Gakkai members are more skeptical; while public officials are generally "mistrusted," the Sōka Gakkai members are even less inclined to trust them, and so on. Thus here, as on other grounds, we are encouraged to conclude that the Sōka Gakkai is not an "un-Japanese" organization, but rather one which appeals to and rallies around it persons who perhaps feel more acutely the dissatisfactions that are prevalent in most of Japanese society.

We inquired at the beginning of this section whether or not the members of the Sōka Gakkai would be "cured" of their postulated social alienation by affiliation with the Sōka Gakkai. By the measures above, we may be led to conclude that, generally speaking, they are not. This is especially true of the "faith-in-people" dimension. But other of the data from Hayasaka and our own study warn us to be careful not to overgeneralize.

We have seen that Sōka Gakkai members come predominantly from lower-educated, lower-income, and lower-occupational categories. Table 11 also shows that women, older persons, and persons who are lower in education, income, and occupation are more alienated than are men, younger persons, and persons in higher educational, income, and occupational status. Thus we are led to inquire how lower- and upper-status Sōka Gakkai members compare in alienation with lower- and

TABLE 11

"ALIENATION SCALE" RESPONSES OF DEMOGRAPHIC CATEGORIES
OF THE 1965 TOKYO SAMPLE
(In Per Cent)

	High Alienation	Low Alienation	Total	(N)
SEX				
Male	25	75	100	(494)
Female	36	64	100	(469)
(N)	(295)	(668)		(963)
AGE				
20–34	27	73	100	(592)
35 and over	37	63	100	(373)
(N)	(296)	(669)		(965)
EDUCATION				
Elementary, Middle	43	57	100	(373)
High, University	22	87	100	(563)
(N)	(283)	(653)		(936)
INCOME				
60,000 yen or less	33	67	100	(494)
Over 60,000 yen	25	75	100	(390)
(N)	(263)	(621)		(884)
OCCUPATION				
Shop, Laborer	38	62	100	(474)
Professional, Managerial, Office	22	78	100	(387)
(N)	(263)	(598)		(861)

(N) = number of cases on which percentages are based.

higher-status nonmembers. Is the greater alienation of the Sōka Gakkai a function of its class composition? Does Sōka Gakkai membership "cure" alienation, or not?

Table 12 shows results of a cross tabulation of four religious categories by sex, age, education, family income, and occupation. We see that Sōka Gakkai members of lower social status, women, and younger members generally score about the same

TABLE 12

Percentage of Demographic Categories in Each Religious
Group of the 1965 Tokyo Sample Scoring High
("alienated") on Alienation Scale
(In Per Cent)

	No Religion	Other Religion	Sōka Gakkai	Christian	(N)
Sex					
Male	24	34	35	33	(125)
Female	36	46	41	9	(171)
Age					
20–34	26	39	30	16	(158)
35 and over	36	41	45	14	(138)
Education					
Elementary, Middle	41	52	45	25	(158)*
High, University	22	26	29	14	(123)
Income					
60,000 yen or less	33	53	28	17	(173)*
Over 60,000 yen	23	29	57	17	(88)
Occupation					
Shop, Laborer	37	49	37	27	(178)†
Professional, Managerial, Office	21	26	50	13	(84)
(N)	(237)	(37)	(17)	(5)	(296)

* Does not total 296 because of "don't know" or refusals.
† Does not total 296 because category not dichotomous.
(N) = number of cases on which percentages are based.

as persons with no religion, while higher-status Sōka Gakkai members, men, and older members score higher (more alienated). In comparison with adherents of "other religions" (except Christians), the record is mixed. In all categories, members of "other religions" are more alienated than Tōkyō citizens of no religion. In some areas (females, younger persons, lower education, income, and occupation) they scored much higher than the Sōka Gakkai, while in others (higher income and occupation), they scored much lower than did Sōka Gakkai members, though higher than nonmembers. The data for Christians, however, are strikingly different in all categories, save for males. Far fewer Christians scored in the "alienated" end of the scale than did persons in other areas.

Thus the data from cross tabulation enable us to conclude that our initial evaluation was probably correct: Sōka Gakkai members generally have value profiles (according to these measures) similar to those of the average nonmember. Sōka Gakkai profiles "bulge" somewhat more in the direction of "alienation" than do the average nonmembers'. But generally the shape is the same. It is only for Christians that we note a strong and consistent difference: Christians in all categories are less alienated than are any other group; the value profiles of Christians are quite different from those of nonreligious Tokyo citizens, Sōka Gakkai members, or members of other religions. Thus, a by-product of our investigation of the Sōka Gakkai is the indication that while the values of lower-status Sōka Gakkai members correspond to those of ordinary lower-status Japanese, those of Japanese Christians at this level are considerably different. Moreover, Christians are far less alienated regardless of social status. Finally, while Hayasaka remarked on the homogeneity of Sōka Gakkai attitudes compared with those of nonmembers, our data indicate that the attitudes of Christians on these items are even more homogeneous.

We conclude, then, that on most social and personal matters, Sōka Gakkai members are seldom "better" and usually are somewhat "worse" than the general population, though often they are no worse, and occasionally they are somewhat better, than are members of either the traditional or the new religions.

IV

THE

FUNCTIONS

AND APPEALS

OF THE

SŌKA GAKKAI

IN ORDER TO HELP make our examination of the Sōka Gakkai something of a contribution to the study of religio-ideological groups generally, before we undertook our research we surveyed reports of other groups which we felt might have elements of similarity to the Sōka Gakkai. We considered especially the following four areas: (1) methods of analysis (looking primarily for studies that used survey data, analysis of members' testimonials, and participant observation); (2) the development of typologies of religio-ideological groups; (3) demographic, behavioral, and attitudinal characteristics of members compared with nonmembers; and (4) the social and personal function of religio-ideological groups.

Our methodological debt is apparent from the bibliography where we list sources we have consulted which have reported on the use primarily of participant observation, survey techniques, and content analysis in the study of religio-ideological groups. Hence, we will turn our attention directly to the question of typology.

Typologies of Religious Groups

In increasing order of difficulty and sophistication, we believe that the application of a scientific method to the study of objects has as its goal the explanation, prediction, and control of the objects under consideration. It is an indication of the primitiveness of most social or behavioral science (in contrast to much natural science, for example) that we have little agreement at the first level (explanation) and virtually none at the other two. Specifically, as far as the study of religio-ideological groups is concerned, we have yet to arrive at a satisfactory agreement concerning that which is generally considered to be the necessary first step in a scientific method—the classification of the objects under study. That is, we do not yet have an exhaustive and generally agreed upon typology of religious groups.

Although the development of various attempts at religious typologies is a familiar story to students of the sociology of religion, since it is our intention systematically to relate our findings about the Sōka Gakkai to the main body of religious research, and since some persons who may be reading our report (specialists of Japanese studies, for example) may have been drawn to it for other reasons than a prior interest in the study of religious groups as such, we believe it is advisable to take the time to describe that development once again.

The basic typology of religious organizations seems to be that of Ernst Troeltsch (and by him from Max Weber).[1] Troeltsch used the simplest possible typology—a dichotomy —by which to classify Christian groups as either churches or sects. Although his dichotomy, as we shall see, has subsequently been expanded into a continuum, nonetheless his formulation remains central to all typologies that we have encountered. According to Troeltsch, a *church* is a religious organization that is conservative, universal in aspiration (and generally actually large in membership), relatively easy to join (most persons are born into it), supportive of this world and its leading in-

[1] Ernst Troeltsch, *The Social Teachings of the Christian Churches* (New York: Macmillan, 1931), I, 331–81. In this section on typology, in addition to the sources cited specifically here, we have relied on various works listed in the bibliography.

stitutions and their incumbents, and hence aligned with and reciprocally dependent upon the controlling elite of the society in which it is located. The church does not encourage its members to reject or alter the institutional or ethical patterns of their society, but rather it encourages them better to conform to the world. It stresses the role of the clergy as preservers and dispensers of God's grace and hence (in Christian terms) of the Sacraments and Tradition.

In contrast to this is the *sect*, which is small and particularistic in membership; difficult to join (generally only adults may enter, and then only after a period of apprenticeship and/or some evidence of divine selection and a somehow changed life); opposed to the institutions, rulers, and ethics of society, either actively and militantly or passively and by withdrawal; and hence composed of persons who are outside of the controlling centers of society. To a greater or lesser extent, it rejects a clergy and objective, impersonal religious formulizations, and emphasizes the role of the laity and their subjective and more personal modes of direct religious experience and expression. The sect makes a sharp distinction between the purity and moral superiority of its sanctified members and the hypocrisy and evil of all those outside its fold.[2]

Troeltsch's dichotomy was expanded to a continuum by Howard Becker, who suggested that religious organizations could better be classified by reference to four ideal types in ascending order of size, universality, and affirmative attitude toward the world: cult, sect, denomination, and ecclesia.

The *cult* is considered to be a community of mystics who do not necessarily formally join the group but who are drawn together by the bond of similar ideas and modes of religious expression.[3] *Sects*, for Becker, are essentially as Troeltsch de-

[2] According to David O. Moberg, *The Church as a Social Institution* (New York: Prentice-Hall, 1962), p. 75, Troeltsch also distinguished a third type, mysticism, which is a mode of purely individualistic and subjective religious expression which rejects any form of religious community, dogma, or liturgy for a strictly personal and immediate communion with the divine.

[3] See Leopold von Weise and Howard Becker, "Four Types of Religious Organization," pp. 624–42 in *Systematic Sociology* (New York: Wiley, 1932). Examples of cults might be Spiritualism, Theosophy, New Thought, Christian Science, Unity, and Buchmanism. These and the following ex-

scribed them, but Elizabeth Nottingham[4] has emphasized the distinction between *withdrawing sects* which, though rejecting the world, are passively oriented to it,[5] and *militant sects* which actively fight against the world (for example, Jehovah's Witnesses). *Denominations* are either sects that have lasted past the first generation, have attracted more prosperous and influential members (or whose members have become successful in this world), and hence have become less opposed to society and more inclusive in membership (Methodists or Baptists), or else they are "reduced" ecclesiae—ecclesiae that circumstances have forced to assume the more modest dimensions of a denomination (Episcopal and Lutheran groups in the United States). The *ecclesia* itself is basically Troeltsch's church (European Lutheran, Anglican, Roman Catholic).

As may be surmised, Becker suggests the idea of religious development along this four-place continuum. The suggestion is that religious groups begin as cults, develop into sects, and thence to denominations, and finally ecclesiae. The movement is neither inevitable nor sequential, however.[6] A group may experience an arrested development and stay at one stage permanently or at least for a very long time; or it may pass rapidly through some stages and linger in others; or it may move backward along the continuum (as when it is transplanted from one environment to another, for example); or it may atrophy and die.

---

amples, however, are from Moberg, *The Church as a Social Institution*, pp. 78–79.

[4] Elizabeth K. Nottingham, *Religion and Society* (New York: Random House, 1954), p. 63.

[5] Examples are medieval monastic orders, Plymouth Brethren, Old Order Amish.

[6] On this point see Peter Berger, "Sectarianism and Religious Sociation," *American Journal of Sociology*, LXIV (July, 1958), 41–44; Thomas F. O'Dea, "Mormonism and the Avoidance of Sectarian Stagnation," *American Journal of Sociology*, LX (November, 1954), 285–93; Harold W. Pfautz, "Christian Science: A Case Study of the Social Psychology Aspect of Secularization," *Social Forces*, XXXIV (March, 1956), 246–51; Pfautz, "The Sociology of Secularization," *American Journal of Sociology*, LXI (July, 1955), 121–28. Byran Wilson, "An Analysis of Sect Development," *American Sociological Review*, XXIV (February, 1959), 3–15; Rex Skidmore, "The Protestant Church and Recreation—An Example of Social Change," *Social Forces*, XX (1947), 364–70.

In any event, the notion both of a continuum and of the development of religious groups along it (with the empirically induced corollary that any actual religious group may not fit precisely into one of the four niches partly because the four categories are ideal types and partly because real religious groups may be under analysis at a time when they are in transition from one type to another) has had considerable influence upon our conceptualization and analysis of religious groups.

There have been a number of further refinements of the developing continuum as described by Becker and his followers. J. Milton Yinger[7] has suggested a six-point scale—cult, sect, established sect, denomination or class church, ecclesia, and universal church—the terms of which, in the light of our presentation of Troeltsch's and Becker's typologies, should be sufficiently clear. What Yinger has done essentially is to broaden the scale through the inclusion of the established sect and universal church categories, enabling empirically observed groups to be categorized better than is possible in a four-fold classification alone.

William Mann, in his study of religious groups in Alberta, Canada,[8] uses only a three-point typology of sect, cult, and church which, as we shall see, nonetheless has certain advantages for our purposes. Mann says that a *church* is accommodated to the secular world, is aligned with the upper and upper-middle classes, is this-worldly, and that membership in the church is a token of respectability in the community. As churches, he includes both the Roman Catholic and Anglican, and the Presbyterian, Methodist, and Baptist.

Sects, Mann suggests, are characterized by an ascetic morality, are other-worldly, reject formality and conventionality in their worship, and believe in the strict interpretation of the scriptures and the correctness of the earliest known practices (i.e., of those who had first-hand contact with the founder or founders). Having a small, culturally homogeneous and highly selective membership and no professional or hierarchal clergy (though leader-

---

[7] J. Milton Yinger, *Religion, Society and the Individual* (New York: Macmillan, 1957), pp. 147–55.

[8] William E. Mann, *Sect, Cult, and Church in Alberta* (Toronto University of Toronto Press, 1955), pp. 5–8.

ship is frequently charismatic), they practice relatively strict equality and fraternity within the group and encourage individual modes of religious expression. The members come from the disadvantaged segments of society and are opposed to the morals and power of the controlling classes. Existing in an environment of rapid social change, they are instruments of social and religious protest, although they may either encourage their members to withdraw from contact with the corrupt world or actively seek to reform it.[9]

As Mann sees them, *cults* are quite different. They are syncretic, blending traditional and alien religions with elements of modern science, and hence are pseudorational and logical, nonemotional, and stress the primacy of mind over matter. They are opposed to extravagant ritual or ceremonial, and have rational, business-like organizations and meetings. Far from rejecting the world, they seek worldly prestige, popularity, and wealth. They accept most of the secular values and help their members the better to achieve them. They have a utilitarian approach to this world, and because of their better knowledge or the possession of some secret information, assume that they are intellectually superior (rather than morally superior as a sect does) to ordinary people. They do not have an antiworldly, ascetic code of ethics, but rather stress harmony, happiness, and success. Membership is relatively easy, and they have a speculative or allegorical interpretation of their scriptures. Leadership is generally rational (in Weber's meaning) rather than charismatic, though it is more likely that a cult will have female leaders than will either a church or a sect.[10]

Several more detailed typologies of sects and cults have been developed which, however, do not seem to us to distinguish between the two as helpfully as Mann does.[11]

[9] Some of Mann's examples of sects are the Salvation Army, the German Baptist Church, the Mennonites, Christadelphians, Church of God, Church of the Nazarene, Disciples of Christ, Foursquare Gospel, the Holiness Movement, Jehovah's Witnesses, and the Seventh-Day Adventists.

[10] His examples of cults include Christian Science, Unity Truth, Theosophy, I Am, Rosicrucianism, Spiritualism, and Divine Science.

[11] Elmer T. Clark, *The Small Sects in America* (Nashville, Tenn.: Abingdon-Cokesbury, 1949), discusses seven types of *sects*: Pessimistic or Adventist (such as Seventh-Day Adventist, Jehovah's Witnesses), Per-

Before evaluating the Sōka Gakkai according to these typologies, we need at least to mention certain other facets of
religious groups that have been suggested as providing criteria
by which to compare and evaluate them. One is the question of
polity. Traditional research into Christian groups has asked
whether the group has an episcopal, presbyterian, or congregational form,[12] although these categories are recognized now as
having very limited usefulness even for Christian organizations.
Similarly, there is the question of the type of leadership. In
Weber's terms, is the group's leadership essentially traditional,
charismatic, or legal-rational?[13] Finally, Joachim Wach[14] has
suggested a typology that centers on the nature of the origin of
the religious group: was it natural (i.e., did it evolve from a
family, kinship, locality, racial, national, sex, or age group?), or
was it founded? If founded, is it a continuation of a brotherhood resulting from the institutionalization of the religious experience of the original founder and his disciples, or is it a
reform or secessionist group from another religious body?[15]

---

fectionist or Subjectivist (Quakers, Holiness, Oxford Group), Charismatic
or Pentecostal (Pentecostal Assemblies, House of Prayer), Communistic
(Shakers, House of David), Legalistic or Objectivistic (Reformed Episcopal, Old Catholic, Seventh-Day Baptist), Egocentric or New Thought
(Christian Science, Unity School), Esoteric or Mystic (I Am, Rosicrucianism, Theosophy).

Peter Berger, "The Sociological Study of Sectarianism," *Social Research*,
XXI (Winter, 1954), 467–85, develops a still more elaborate typology
of sects and cults according to the nature of the group's religious experience and message, attitude toward the world, type, and motif. See his
chart on page 478. He also suggests that each religious group be studied
according to its attitudes toward reality, eschatology, apologetics, and
lack of faith.

[12] For examples of this older approach, see William J. Seabury, *An
Introduction to the Study of Ecclesiastical Polity* (New York: Crothers &
Korth, 1894) and Samuel Wallis, *Synopsis of Lectures on Church Polity*
(Alexandria, Va.: R. Bell's Sons, 1904).

[13] Max Weber, *From Max Weber, Essays in Sociology* (New York:
Oxford University Press, 1946).

[14] Joachim Wach, *Sociology of Religion* (Chicago, Ill.: University of
Chicago Press, 1944).

[15] Since our interest in the Sōka Gakkai is in the sociopolitical activities
of its members and not primarily in their beliefs (though we recognize
that belief and action are of course closely related), we omit here the
consideration of typologies which classify religions principally by reference
to their beliefs. For examples of such classifications of the new religions
in Japan, with some reference to the Sōka Gakkai, see Clark B. Offner

Now we are in a position to attempt to categorize the Sōka Gakkai according to the various typologies that we have presented. Consideration of the church-sect typologies leads us to conclude that the Sōka Gakkai at present is surely neither an ecclesia, a church, nor a denomination. Rather, it can best be typed as a *cult*, especially if we adopt William Mann's designation of a cult in contrast to a sect.

The Sōka Gakkai, while based on the Nichiren Shōshū tradition of Japanese Buddhism, interprets its scriptures rather loosely and allegorically. Its teachings are a syncretic blending of traditional dogma and modern science, and its over-all tone is consistently pseudoscientific. Without denying the reality of matter, as we have seen, the Sōka Gakkai nonetheless stresses the superiority of mind over matter. Its organization and meetings (if we consider the Sōka Gakkai apart from Nichiren Shōshū itself) are businesslike and rational. It professes no ascetic morality, but rather adopts contemporary Japanese morals, and encourages its members to succeed within current Japanese society. Hence, it is wholly this-worldly, virtually lacking any form of eschatology. While it certainly seeks to transform the world, it is a transformation according to goals (if not means) that are generally acceptable to most Japanese and, indeed, most Westerners (for example, the end of war, misery, poverty, sickness, natural disasters, corrupt government, and the establishment of a peaceful, happy, and prosperous world where each person is encouraged to pursue his own interests). Membership is open to anyone who cares to join—indeed, attempts at recruiting members (*shakubuku*) are, we have seen, the main activities of Sōka Gakkai members.

Leadership is more nearly rational-technological than either charismatic (although we have seen that President Ikeda and former President Toda did possess some charismatic qualities) or traditional (though this is found in the priestly leadership of Nichiren Shōshū itself). Moreover while Nichiren Shōshū, at this stage in history and for many non–Sōka Gakkai Japa-

---

and Henry Van Straelen, *Modern Japanese Religions* (New York: Twayne Publishers, 1963), especially pp. 98–109, and Harry Thomsen, *The New Religions of Japan* (Rutland, Vt.: Charles E. Tuttle, 1963), especially pp. 81–108.

nese, relates to Wach's typologies according to origin as a
natural (racial-nationality) group, the Sōka Gakkai itself is
a founded organization which, though huge (its enormous size
makes the "cult" designation somewhat peculiar), nonetheless
is close enough in time to its founder (Makiguchi) and so far
free from schism that it can be called a cult-type brotherhood
resulting from the institutionalization of the religious expression of the original founder and his disciples.

Thus, in spite of its great size and its aggressive conversion
techniques, we conclude that the Sōka Gakkai fits most nearly
the requirements of a cult, and that its obvious parallels with
other cults, especially Christian Science, New Thought, and
the Oxford Movement,[16] should be stressed.

Now we need to reintroduce another point which loomed
large in our earlier discussion of the Sōka Gakkai and which we
have so far not mentioned in this discussion of typologies. That
aspect is the relationship of the demographic, behavioral, and
attitudinal characteristics of ordinary American or Japanese
Sōka Gakkai members to those found in various other religious
groups.

Demographic and Attitudinal Characteristics of Religious and Nonreligious Persons and Groups According to Western Research

We need to know first whether or not behavioral research
has discovered consistent and significant demographic, behavioral, and attitudinal differences between members of religious
groups and persons who are not members. If differences have
been found, we need further to know what they are and

[16] See Charles S. Braden, *They Also Believe* (New York: Macmillan,
1960), chaps. v (Christian Science), iii (New Thought), and xii (Oxford
Movement); as well as Pfautz, "Christian Science"; R. W. England,
"Some Aspects of Christian Science as Reflected in the Letters of
Testimony," *American Journal of Sociology*, LIX (March, 1954), 448–53;
A. W. Eister, *Drawing Room Conversion: A Sociological Study of the
Oxford Group Movement* (Durham, N.C.: Duke University Press, 1950);
Walter H. Clark, *The Oxford Group* (New York: Bookman Associates,
1951); and Alfred W. Griswold, "New Thought: A Cult of Success,"
American Journal of Sociology, XL (November, 1934), 309–18.

whether they are culture-specific or not. That is, in this last regard, are they differences that can be expected to occur wherever religious groups are found, or are they peculiar to certain times and places?

Second, whether or not we find differences between religious affiliates and nonaffiliates generally, are there significant variations between members of the different religious groups? If so, can these be attributed primarily to varying dogmatic features (creeds, polities, ethical rules, etc.) between the groups, or can these dogmatic differences be factored out; that is, can they be explained by reference to other demographic or attitudinal group correlates?

Although now ten years old, and based upon data somewhat older, Michael Argyle's *Religious Behaviour*,[17] a compilation of works on the social psychology of religion conducted in England and America in the twentieth century, remains the best single point of departure in our search for information about demographic, behavioral, and attitudinal differences between members and nonmembers of religious groups. Painting the picture in very crude strokes indeed, we might summarize Argyle's evaluations as follows.

1. *Demographic differences.* First we will consider the demographic data which Argyle presents.

a. *Age.* There seem to be sufficient differences of religious belief and affiliation between the age groups to conclude that there is something that might be called a U-shaped life cycle: children tend to be quite religious, though the content of their beliefs is fairy-taleish and literal. From adolescence to middle age, religious beliefs and affiliation decline sharply; thereafter, they markedly rise till they reach their peak in old age where beliefs in God, heaven, and the like are almost universally held (chap. vi).

b. *Sex.* Women are far more religious than men, whether measured by church membership, orthodoxy of beliefs, or saying prayers (chap. vii).

c. *Marital status.* Persons who are widowed tend to be the most actively and devoutly religious of any marital category,

---

[17] Michael Argyle, *Religious Behaviour* (London: Routledge & Kegan Paul, 1958).

and married people the least. Single and divorced people hold an intermediate position, but single people are more likely to be members of churches than are divorced people. However, the data on marital status and religion are so interlaced with intervening variables as to be highly suspect (pp. 123–24).

d. *Education.* Although Argyle's information on the relation between level of education and religious beliefs and activities is rather fragmentary, it appears that persons with lower levels of education are more religious than persons at the highest levels (pp. 42–46). Persons with higher intelligence and achievement are also less likely to be religious than are those with lower IQs (pp. 92–96).

e. *Social class.* The evidence presented concerning social class also most certainly does not seem to be conclusive to us, but there does seem to be some tendency for middle- and upper-middle-class persons to be *more* religious than are either the upper or lower classes (pp. 129–33).[18]

f. *Minority groups.* Members of minority groups are usually more religious than is the general population, and they tend to belong to sectarian groups that reject this world in often violent terms (pp. 133–34).

g. *Urban-rural differences.* Religious affiliation and beliefs are more prevalent among persons in rural than in urban areas (pp. 134–35).

h. *Parental influences.* There is sufficient evidence to conclude that persons whose parents were religious are more likely to be religious themselves (and to have beliefs and affiliations similar to those of their parents) than are people whose parents were not religious. The beliefs of one's mother seem to be more influential than are those of one's father (pp. 39–42).

i. No specific data are given by Argyle precisely concerning the relationship between *income* and *occupation* (two other demographic variables we related to membership in the Sōka

---

[18] Katherine and Charles George, "Roman Catholic Sainthood and Social Status: A Statistical and Analytical Study," *Journal of Religion*, XXXV (Spring, 1955), 85–98, discovered that from the first through the twentieth centuries, 78 per cent of all Roman Catholic saints have been from the upper classes, 17 per cent from the middle classes, and 5 per cent from the lower classes, although the class composition of society has been almost the opposite of this throughout most of the time.

Gakkai), but they are mentioned in his discussion of social class and seem to be related more to specific denominational membership than to the presence or absence of religious affiliation and activities themselves.

2. *Mental health.* Since our study of Sōka Gakkai respondents and their testimonials showed that Sōka Gakkai members manifested a considerable number of emotional problems from which the Gohonzon granted relief, we should also consider the available evidence on the relationship between religious beliefs and mental health. Argyle displays the data concerning neurosis and psychosis separately.

Concerning neurosis, Argyle summarizes the evidence as showing that there is more neurosis among religious persons between the ages of sixteen and thirty than there is among nonreligious persons of the same ages; religious orthodoxy correlates with anxiety and ego defensiveness; and among older people, the religious are better adjusted than are the nonreligious (pp. 102–7). Concerning psychosis, however, there is no evidence that religious persons are clearly more or less psychotic, or that psychotics are more or less religious, though roughly over one in seven psychotic patients manifests a decidedly religious content in his psychotic behavior (pp. 107–9).

Finally, concerning the question of whether religion is the cause or the cure of mental illness, Argyle concludes that there is really no evidence which demonstrates that religion produces mental disorder (p. 117), though some people, such as hysterics, worsen considerably when they are subjected to revivalistic religious situations. Moreover, he says that the evidence does not enable us to decide definitely whether or not religion decreases mental illness (pp. 117–19), although it does seem to decrease it for older persons.

Thus, we cannot determine the causal relation between religion and mental health. Indeed, we cannot even conclude that the two are unrelated (p. 119).[19]

[19] See also Walter H. Clark, *The Psychology of Religion* (New York: Macmillan, 1958); Ernest Harms, "Religious Conversion, Mental Health, and Priestly Responsibility," *Religious Education*, LIV (May–June, 1959), 217–22; Harms, "Ethical and Psychological Implications of Religious Conversion," *Review of Religious Research*, III (1962), 122–30; Robert J. Kleiner *et al.*, "Mental Disorder and Status Based on Religious Affilia-

3. *Sexual activity and religion.* The relation between sexual activities and beliefs and religiosity is somewhat clearer, however. Religious persons report fewer incidents of masturbation, fewer orgasms per week, less homosexuality, less premarital intercourse, and somewhat less frequency and satisfaction of marital intercourse than do nonreligious persons, but these differences were found more directly related to social class than to religion (pp. 121–23). Persons who were religious were more opposed to divorce, birth control, and premarital sex than were nonreligious persons (p. 126). Finally, religious people report happier marriages than do nonreligious persons, and when husband and wife are of the same religion, the level of satisfaction is considerably higher (pp. 24–26).

Both Argyle and Wallin[20] suggest that although religious activity may provide an effective substitute for sexual gratification, especially among women, still it cannot be concluded that religion either is or is not the cause of these attitudes toward and practices of sex.

4. *Attitudinal differences.* Finally, we can turn our attention to attitudinal differences between religious and nonreligious persons. Argyle's survey of existing religious research leads him to conclude that members of religious groups are less likely to be interested or participant in politics, are more conservative

tion," *Human Relations,* XII (August, 1959), 273–76; Warner Lowe, "Religious Beliefs and Religious Delusions," *American Journal of Psychotherapy,* IX (1955), 54–61; Paul Maves, "Conversion—a Behavioral Category," *Review of Religious Research,* V (1964), 41–50; Wayne Oates, *Religious Dimensions of Personality* (New York: Association Press, 1957); Oates, *Religious Factors in Mental Illness* (New York: Association Press, 1955); Russell Olt, *An Approach to the Psychology of Religion* (Boston, Mass.: Christopher, 1956); Orlo Strunk, Jr. (ed.), *Readings in the Psychology of Religion* (New York: Abingdon, 1959); Leslie D. Weatherhead, *Psychology, Religion, and Healing* (New York: Abingdon, 1952); Elsa Whalley, "Religion and Suicide," *Review of Religious Research,* V (1964), 91–111.

Mason Schall and Jerome Beker, "A Comparison of Religious Beliefs of Delinquent and Non-Delinquent Protestant Adolescent Boys," *Religious Education,* LIX (May–June, 1964), 250–52, found that only on three items of a fifty-three-item inventory of religious beliefs were there any differences between delinquent and nondelinquent boys. On all three, the delinquent gave more rigorously orthodox answers than did the nondelinquents.

[20] Paul Wallin, "Religiosity, Sexual Gratification, and Marital Satisfaction," *American Sociological Review,* XXII (1957), 300–5.

ideologically, are more racially prejudiced (though the more devout or religiously active are less prejudiced) are more suggestible, and more authoritarian than are nonreligious people (pp. 80–92).

5. *Evaluation of differences between religious and nonreligious groups.* While we can conclude that there do appear to be some significant differences between religious and nonreligious persons, we are as yet unable to determine whether religious belief is the causal element in these relationships, the result of the demographic, behavioral, and attitudinal factors, or whether the items are only spuriously related.[21]

Moreover, we asked above whether these empirically discovered correlations between the various items and religion are culture-specfic or not. Unfortunately, because there has been so little empirically based and methodologically comparable studies conducted in non–Anglo-Saxon (much less non-Western and non-Christian) areas, we are not able to answer our

[21] Among the more recent attempts to discover a relationship between religiosity and personality characteristics are Joseph Faulkner and Gordon DeJong, "Religiosity in 5-D: An Empirical Analysis," *Social Forces*, XLV (December, 1966), 246–54; Jack Frymier, "Relationship Between Church Attendance and Authoritarianism," *Religious Education*, LIV (July–August, 1959), 369–71; Seward Hiltner and William Rogers, "Research on Religion and Personality Dynamics," *Religious Education*, LVII (July–August, 1962), S-128–S-140; Bernard Lazerwitz, "Some Factors Associated with Variations in Church Attendance," *Social Forces*, XXXIX (May, 1961), 301–9; John Photiadis and Jeanne Bigger, "Religiosity, Education, and Ethnic Distance," *American Journal of Sociology*, LXVII (1962), 666–72; Photiadis and A. L. Johnson, "Orthodoxy, Church Participation, and Authoritarianism," *American Journal of Sociology*, LXIX (November, 1963), 244–48; Snell Putney and Russell Middleton, "Dimension and Correlates of Religious Ideology," *Social Forces*, XXXIX (May, 1961), 285–90; Bernard Spilka and James Reynolds, "Religion and Prejudice: A Factor-Analytic Study," *Review of Religious Research*, VI (1965), 163–67; Frederick Whitam, "Subdimensions of Religiosity and Race Prejudice," *Review of Religious Research*, III (1962), 166–74; John Wright, "Personal Adjustment and Its Relation to Religious Attitudes and Certainty," *Religious Education*, LIV (November–December, 1959), 521–23.

Hans Toch and Robert Anderson, "Religious Belief and Denominational Affiliation," *Religious Education*, LV (May–June, 1960), 193–200, argue that knowledge of a person's denominational affiliation gives little clue as to his religious beliefs, but this contention is specifically rejected by Carl Poit, "A Study Concerning Religious Belief and Denominational Affiliation," *Religious Education*, LVII (May–June, 1962), 214–16.

question. We will hazard the guess, however, that these differences we noted between religious and nonreligious persons will tend to be found in most modern or industrially advanced countries, regardless of their religious orientation, but not in traditional or developing areas. Hence, we can expect that (generally speaking) they would be found to apply to Japan, or at least in Tokyo and other urban areas of Japan.

6. *Differences between religious groups themselves.* The final major question we asked above was whether demographic, behavioral, and attitudinal differences found between religious and nonreligious persons were greater than those found among the various Judeo-Christian groups themselves. Although a full summary of all the data relating to this question would take us far from the main focus of our study, and while the qualifications and exceptions we should make are many indeed, the general thrust of the data, it seems to us, is that between-religious-group demographic, behavioral, and attitudinal differences are as great as those found between religious and nonreligious persons generally.

Many, but not all, studies show significant differences in the three areas of characteristics we have surveyed. Generally speaking, Christian denominations in the United States can be ranked (according to socioeconomic status, level of education, income, occupation, political conservatism, and so forth) from Episcopal, Presbyterian, and Congregational at the top, Lutheran and Methodist at the middle, Baptist and Roman Catholic near the bottom, and Protestant fundamentalistic sects at the bottom. Jews are found to be high in education, income, and occupation, but low in authoritarianism, conservatism, and status. Cults tend to attract persons of upper status, better education, and higher income, have more women than men and persons of middle age than younger persons. They are politically conservative and authoritarian.[22]

[22] See W. and B. Allinsmith, "Religious Affiliation and Politico-economic Attitude," *Public Opinion Quarterly*, XII (1948), 377–89; Argyle, *Religious Behavior*, chaps. viii and xi; Donald Matthews, *United States Senators and Their World* (New York: Vintage Books, 1960), pp. 23–24; John Schmidhauser, "The Justices of the Supreme Court," *Midwest Journal of Political Science*, III (1959), 22; Liston Pope, "Religion and the Class Structure," *The Annals*, CCLVI (1948), pp. 84–91.

While other attitudinal, behavioral, and demographic differences have been found between Roman Catholics and all Protestants, race and class seem to be strongly influential—if not actually controlling—intervening variables here.[23]

Thus, we are led to conclude that while we do find significant differences between various religious groups and between members and nonmembers, we cannot say that religious faith itself either is or is not a prime causal agent of the observed differences. While extant reports of empirical studies of religions are helpful first steps, if we are to develop a truly cross-cultural, and hence more nearly scientific, understanding of religio-ideological groups, far more extensive, methodologically comparable, and better financed studies than we have at present are needed.

Evaluation of the Characteristics of Sōka Gakkai Members

In spite of these reservations, and in spite of the necessity of repeating our earlier warning that we are not able to use the data on Judeo-Christian groups to prove or disprove our information on the Sōka Gakkai specifically or Tokyo citizens generally, we feel it is very worthwhile to compare our findings in this study with those which we have just summarized above.

1. *Demographic characteristics.* It is striking how similar are the two sets of findings concerning demographic characteristics. Generally speaking, in our Tokyo sample (see Table 9), religious persons are in greater proportion women, older, less well educated, and widowed. The proportion of single persons is also lower than it is for nonreligious people. However, even greater than the differences between religious and nonreligious persons were the differences between the various Japanese religious groups. The demographic characteristics might be charted as in Table 13.

Thus we can conclude that in Japan as in the West there are significant demographic differences between religious and

[23] See especially Gerhard Lenski, *The Religious Factor* (Garden City, N.Y.: Doubleday, 1963), *passim.*

TABLE 13

SUMMARY OF THE DEMOGRAPHIC CHARACTERISTICS OF RELIGIOUS GROUPS IN THE TOYKO SURVEY

	No Religion	All Religions	Traditional Religions	New Religions	Sōka Gakkai	Christians
Sex	about equal	slightly more women	slightly more women	somewhat more women	about equal	overwhelmingly more women
Age	about equal	⅔ more over 35	overwhelmingly older	¾ more over 35	½ over 35	⅔ *under* 35
Marital Status	⅔ married ⅓ single	⅔ married ⅙ widowed ⅙ single	⅔ married ⅕ widowed few single	⅔ married ⅙ widowed ⅙ single	⅔ married ⅙ widowed or divorced ⅕ single	½ married ½ single
Education	⅔ higher	equal high and low	equal high and low	⅔ low	equal high and low	9/10 high
Income	½ low	equal high and low	⅔ high	½ low	⅘ low	⅔ high
Occupation	½ low	½ low	½ low	½ high	¾ low	½ high
Class	⅕ low	⅕ low	⅙ low	¼ low	½ low	1/20 low

nonreligious persons, but that of even greater importance are the differences between the various religious groups. To say that a person is a member of a religious organization is to indicate the probability of his being somewhat different from nonreligious persons on certain demographic factors, but it is not nearly as significant as indicating what his particular religious affiliation is. Most important, it is not at all clear that purely religious factors (i.e., matters of faith or dogma) are the causal agents behind these differences.

2. *Social attitudes*. But what is the case as far as attitudes are concerned? Here also the circumstances seem roughly similar to those found in the West. Our religious respondents generally displayed *slightly* less "desirable" personality attributes on the five-scale measures we used (see Table 10), but again, the denominational differences were far greater than those found simply between religious and nonreligious persons. Religious persons were slightly more authoritarian, anomic, had less faith in people, and a lower sense of citizen's duty, though they had slightly less mistrust of public officials. None of these differences was statistically significant, however. The situation was quite different when we looked at the various religious groupings: Christians were uniformly at the more "desirable" ends of every scale, and the Sōka Gakkai and new religions more frequently at the "undesirable" ends, though these two groups themselves often differed on specific scales.

3. *Attitudes toward sex*. Although we had no questions in our survey about our respondents' sexual experiences, so that we cannot compare religious and nonreligious persons on this dimension, we did have one item that gives us some small indication of our respondents' attitudes toward sex. We asked them to agree or disagree with the statement that it was all right for women to have premarital sexual experiences. All categories of respondents strongly disagree, and there was only a slight and statistically insignificant difference between religious and nonreligious persons: 15 per cent of the former said it was all right compared to 17 per cent of the latter. There were not many differences between the religious groups themselves, except that only 7 per cent of the Christians agreed, which was the lowest percentage of any group, while 19 per

cent of the members of traditional religions said it was all right. Thus, generally, the data substantiate a point we have made before[24] that Japanese as a whole do not have a permissive attitude toward sex, although there are some groups who are more liberal than others.

4. *Marital satisfaction.* Another factor about which the Western religious data showed differences between religious and nonreligious persons was marital satisfaction—religious persons saying that they are more happily married than do nonreligious persons. We tapped something akin to this when we asked our respondents to say whether they thought their spouse's understanding of them was excellent, good, fair, poor, or bad (pp. 85–86). There was no great difference between the answers of religious and nonreligious persons (31 per cent of the former and 36 per cent of the latter said that understanding was good or excellent). Among the various religious groups, however, there were some variations. Only 26 per cent of the members of the traditional religions and 28 per cent of the Sōka Gakkai members said it was good or excellent, while 35 per cent of the Christians and 39 per cent of the members of the new religions chose these replies. In any event, we do not seem to find here the significantly better understanding that religious people in the West tend to indicate.

5. *Parental influence.* Finally, Western studies show that one's parents, especially his mother, are most important in determining whether or not a person will have any religion at all, regardless of what it is. We found both of these points to be the case with our respondents as well (pp. 88–92). Except for the members of the new religions, religious persons tend to come from religious families, while, except for Christians, the role of the mother seems to be somewhat more important than that of the father. Hence we can conclude that our data about demographic, behavioral, and attitudinal differences between religious and nonreligious persons, and between persons of different religions, are roughly similar to those found in the West among (primarily) Judeo-Christian groups.

[24] James Allen Dator, "Life History and Attitudes of Japanese High Court Judges," *Western Political Quarterly*, XX (June, 1967), pp. 408–39.

6. *Reconsideration of the typological identification of the Sōka Gakkai.* We can now return to the point we left hanging at the end of our discussion about the typological designation of the Sōka Gakkai. We had concluded that, on many counts, the Sōka Gakki could be typed as a cult, but we now see that the demographic and attitudinal characteristics of the Sōka Gakkai members are more like those of sectarian affiliates.

In the West, cults tend to have more women than men, while there is typically no sex ratio imbalance for sects; cult members are older, relatively well educated, rather well-to-do, of upper- or middle-status occupation and social class, and less likely to be alienated or anomic. Sect members are young or middle aged, poorly educated, economically poor, of lower status, occupation, and class, and alienated.[25] On all these measures, both American and Japanese members are definitely like sectarian members in the West (while, interestingly, Japanese Christians are more like cult adherents).[26]

This is probably one of the reasons why the Sōka Gakkai has been so perplexing to Western observers, and why it has been

[25] In addition to the general texts on the sociology of religion, and other works cited above, see William Catton, Jr., "What Kind of People Does a Religious Cult Attract," *American Sociological Review*, XXII (October, 1957), 561–66; Russell Dynes, "Church-Sect Typologies and Socio-economic Status," *American Sociological Review*, XX (1955), 555–60; Howard Elinson, "The Implications of Pentecostal Religions for Intellectualism, Politics, and Race Relations," *American Journal of Sociology*, LXX (January, 1965), 403–15; Thomas Ford, "Status, Residence, and Fundamentalist Religious Beliefs in the Southern Appalachians," *Social Forces*, XXXIX (October, 1960), 41–49; Ford, "Religious Thought and Belief in the Southern Appalachians," *Review of Religious Research*, III (1962), 2–20; Allen Jackson, "Religious Beliefs and Experiences of the Southern Highlander," *Review of Religious Research*, III (1962), 21–40; Benton Johnson, "Ascetic Protestantism and Political Preference," *Public Opinion Quarterly*, XXVI (Spring, 1962), 35–46; Johnson, "Ascetic Protestantism and Political Preference in the Deep South," *American Journal of Sociology*, LIX (June, 1964), 359–66; John Lofland and Rodney Stark, "Becoming a World-Saver: A Theory of Conversion to a Deviant Perspective," *American Sociological Review*, XXX (December, 1965), 862–74; Everett Perry, "Socio-Economic Factors and American Fundamentalism," *Review of Religious Research*, I (1960), 57–60; Leslie Sargent, "Occupational Status in a Religious Group," *Review of Religious Research*, IV (1963), 149–54.

[26] In addition to the material in our study, we base this comment on data displayed by Fumio Ikado, "Komyunitei Chiyachi to Taishū Kōzō no Mondai," *Shūkyō Kōron,* XXXI (November, 1961), 8–14.

characterized as a cross between Christian Science (a cult) and Jehovah's Witnesses (a sect):[27] it has the structural and dogmatic features of a cult and the sociological features of a sect. Unfortunately, we cannot resolve this dilemma and we will conclude that this is precisely what the Sōka Gakkai is—a sect-cult.

This designation is not as worthless as it might sound, as it helps explain some of the problems we have touched upon elsewhere in this study. We have shown considerable differences between Sōka Gakkai media-projected images of Japanese members and the data about Sōka Gakkai members gotten from survey research; we have indicated the lofty ideas of the leadership and compared them with those of the members (especially in the area of *shakubuku*); we suggested the generation gaps between the original founder and followers of the Sōka Gakkai, the postwar leaders and followers, and the current mass membership; and we also described the gap between the American leaders and followers on the one hand and the current Japanese leaders on the other.

In all these areas, perhaps, we can see the sect-cult tension operating: the Sōka Gakkai projects a cult message and image, but attracts sectarian persons because of its conversion techniques. The founders (Makiguchi *et al.*) and earliest members were clearly cult-oriented, but the postwar leaders (Toda and friends) and members were sectarian. The current membership is largely sectarian, but the increasingly well-educated and prosperous leadership is cultish, not to say almost denominational. Both the American leaders and followers, however, are sectarian—there is no doubt about this—and so are their Japanese wives, but the Japanese leadership they are in contact with are not.

Hence, the Sōka Gakkai is a blend—so far a successful blend —of sect and cult. Its future development seems generally along the lines of an incipient denomination. If the Japanese nation retains its current growth toward genuine middle-class oriented prosperity, we can expect the denominational features

[27] See "War of the Sects," *Newsweek*, LXVII (March 7, 1966), 86: "Soka Gakkai looks like an Oriental blend of Christian Science and the John Birch Society."

of the Sōka Gakkai to continue to develop and the sectarian features to fade. If world war or world depression should end Japan's economic growth, then the sectarian predilections of its members, who are decidedly opposed to the incumbents of the present power structure (see the responses on the "Mistrust of Public Officials" and especially "Faith in People" scales, Table 10), might overwhelm the more moderate positions of the Sōka Gakkai leaders.

Now we are ready to examine the fourth question we asked at the beginning of this chapter—what are the social and personal functions of religio-ideological groups generally and of the Sōka Gakkai in particular?

The Social and Personal Functions of the Sōka Gakkai

1. *The functional theory of religion.* In preparation for an examination of the appeals of the Sōka Gakkai for its members, we need to ask what the function of religion is for a society and for the individual. To phrase the question in this way is to go a long way toward suggesting an answer to it. For without entering into an argument about the truth of any religious, ideological, or philosophical view, we assume that human beliefs, actions, and institutions can be considered to be components of a social system which has as its basic goal its own preservation. This goal is realized by a component-interaction-ary process by which the total social system is maintained in a dynamic equilibrium.

Following the four cells of nested levels of systems that Talcott Parsons has developed,[28] we see that religious systems

[28] See Talcott Parsons, "The Theoretical Development of the Sociology of Religion," *Journal of the History of Ideas,* V (1944), 176–90; Parsons, *The Social System* (Glencoe, Ill.: Free Press, 1951); Parsons, *Toward a General Theory of Action* (Cambridge, Mass.: Harvard University Press, 1954); Parsons, *Structure and Process in Modern Societies* (Glencoe, Ill.: Free Press, 1960); Parsons et al. (eds.), *Theories of Society* (2 vols.; New York: Free Press of Glencoe, 1961); Parsons, *Social Structure and Personality* (New York: Free Press of Glencoe, 1964). See also Max Black (ed.), *The Social Theories of Talcott Parsons* (Englewood Cliffs, N.J.: Prentice-Hall, 1961) and William Mitchell, *Social Analysis and Politics—The Theories of Talcott Parsons* (Englewood Cliffs, N.J.: Prentice-Hall, 1967).

(institutions, groups, beliefs) fall primarily in the pattern-maintenance sector of a social system, and that religion, hence, has as its primary function, at the societal level, the preservation of the social system, and at the individual level (along with the family and other socializing institutions), the development and inculcation of values which enable the individual to be an effectively functioning member of his society and some sub-group within it.

The values developed and propagated by religious institutions generally have two aspects. One may be called the theological, whereby the basic and apparently unanswerable questions facing the individual (such as the purpose of life, the meaning of death, the creation of the world, etc.) are answered. The second set of values, the ethical, concern inter-personal and intercomponent relations, and establish norms (or ways of determining norms) of proper perception, belief, and action for the various situations in which people find themselves.[29]

In a broad sense, then, the function of the Sōka Gakkai is no different from that of any religio-ideological group. Nor is the function essentially different for American society and American believers than it is for Japanese society and Japanese believers. In both social systems the Sōka Gakkai seeks to provide serviceable theological and ethical guidelines.

But this general statement of the function of religion seems not to enable us to understand the role of the various types of religious groups we have distinguished above, or that of the Sōka Gakkai itself. Especially, it seems to ignore the fact that both sects and cults seem to be *opposed* to their society and to appeal to persons who are alienated from it. We shall show that we do not believe that there is, in fact, a contradiction here, nor that the general functional theory explains only the roles of denominations, churches, or ecclesiae. We believe that reference to the "relative deprivation" theory (and the "contemporary revitalization" theory) and to the types of values which sects and cults espouse, vis-à-vis those of the culture in

[29] Both the liturgical and social aspects of religion we consider to be special cases of the ethical.

which they exist, will show that they are in accord with the functional theory as we sketched it here.

2. *The relative deprivation theory and the Sōka Gakkai.* David Aberle has developed a convenient statement of the relative deprivation theory as it relates to the development of cults which will greatly help us in our understanding of the Sōka Gakkai. A person's feelings of relative deprivation, Aberle says, is the result of a negative and subjectively defined discrepancy between his legitimate status, economic, behavioral, and/or evaluative expectations and his actual situation.[30] His point of reference might be his past versus his present situation, his present versus his future (anticipated) circumstances, or his own versus others' circumstances. Hence, his sense of deprivation might or might not be the result of an actual change in his situation; it might well be simply the result of a change in his perception of or orientation toward his situation (here we also see the similarity of the deprivation theory to that expressed by the phrase, "the revolution of rising expectations").

Attempts to alleviate this sense of relative deprivation can be diverse. They can be individual or group, organized or unorganized, random or planned, active or passive. The individual can join with others in a concerted attempt to get what he wants by means either accepted as legal by the larger society or considered by it to be criminal; he can try to change the world, or somehow transcend the world, or in effect withdraw from the world. He can be active, or apathetic, or suicidal. He can be hopeful or full of despair.

According to our present level of knowledge, says Aberle, we are not able to predict which alternative an individual or a group that feels deprived will take. Thus, mere knowledge of an individual's sense of relative deprivation does not enable us to predict his mode of response, but, Aberle feels, it does enable us to understand the sociopsychological roots behind these various types of responses.

[30] David Aberle, "A Note on Relative Deprivation Theory as Applied to Millenarian and Other Cult Movements," in William A. Lessa and Evan Vogt (eds.), *Reader in Comparative Religion* (New York: Harper and Row, 1965), p. 538.

Vittorio Lanternari also is concerned with this same problem, and uses a similar theory to explain the rise of a great variety of modern messianic cults throughout the world.[31] Messianic cults involve

a belief in [the necessity of] society's return to its source, usually expressed in terms of the expectation of the millennium and the cataclysms and catastrophes that are to precede it, and also embody a belief in the rising of the dead, in the reversal of the existing social order, in the ejection of the white man, in an end of the world, and in its regeneration in an age of abundance and happiness.[32]

The existence of such cults is brought about, says Lanternari, by the interaction of a leader and a cultural crisis, the latter of which may be itself the result of the impact of Western civilization on a primitive culture, or *as in Japan*,[33] war and cultural disintegration, or internal decay and conflict. While there are both endogenous and exogenous causes, there must be a severe value crisis to which the cult is a response: ". . . all the endogenous messianic movements, regardless of their cultural level, are impelled by their nature to escape from society and from the world in order to establish a society and a world of their own beyond history, beyond reality, and beyond the necessity of fighting to bring about change and improvement." [34]

James H. Laue[35] similarly uses A. F. C. Wallace' concept of a revitalization movement[36] to analyze the Black Muslims in America. Laue points out that the Black Muslims, in common with other revitalization movements, are nativistic (seek to eliminate alien persons, customs, and values), revivalistic (seek to reinstitute old—real or imagined—values and customs), vi-

[31] Vittorio Lanternari, *The Religions of the Oppressed: A Study of Modern Messianic Cults* (New York: Alfred A. Knopf, 1963).

[32] *Ibid.*, p. 303.

[33] *Ibid.*, p. 306.

[34] *Ibid.*, p. 314.

[35] James H. Laue, "Contemporary Revitalization Movements in Race Relations: The 'Black Muslims.'" *Social Forces*, XLII (March, 1964), 315–23. See also C. Eric Lincoln, *The Black Muslims in America* (Boston: Beacon Press, 1961) and E. U. Essien-Udom, *Black Nationalism: A Search for Identity in America* (New York: Dell, 1964).

[36] A. F. C. Wallace, "Revitalization Movements," *American Anthropologist*, LVIII (March, 1956), 264–81.

talistic (nonetheless are strongly influenced by the customs, values, and material of the culture they seek to reject), millenarian, and messianic.[37]

We do not contend that the Sōka Gakkai is, strictly speaking, a messianic or millenarian group. There are sufficient points of similarity, however, to merit our comment, we believe.

The Sōka Gakkai began in a period (1937) and in a society (Japan) which had for at least seventy years been experiencing value-disruptive impact from a foreign culture (the West). Though it can, we believe, truthfully be objected that Japan before the Second World War never suffered such extreme dislocations as were experienced by other areas which produced messianic cults (such as the Peyote cults of the American Indian, the cargo cults in Melanesia, or the nativistic-religious movements in Africa and South America), yet it is helpful to regard the Sōka Gakkai, and other pre-war new Japanese religions (and indeed state Shintō itself) as revitalistic movements of some significance.

There can be little doubt, however, that the Second World War and the Occupation resulted in a thoroughgoing crisis in cultural and personal values which produced the situation known in Japan as "the rush-hour of the Gods," [38] and was one force (others including skillful leadership, rational organization, and luck) which lay behind the tremendous postwar growth of the Sōka Gakkai, and perhaps of some of the other religio-ideological groups in Japan as well.

This cultural crisis might have been resolved by complete and protracted mass apathy, or by widespread suicide, or by spontaneous or organized resistance to the Occupation. Although these responses were shown for short periods or by certain persons and groups, they were neither the general nor the lasting reaction. Rather, the Japanese appear to have engaged in a many-faceted group-oriented attempt to re-establish meaning for their lives.[39] Most lost (or found) themselves by

[37] Laue, "Contemporary Revitalization Movements," p. 319.

[38] Raymond Hammer, *Japan's Religious Ferment* (London: SCM Press, 1961), chap. ix.

[39] This virtually complete identification of the individual with one of a variety of groups has considerable historical precedent. We developed this point in considerable detail in an earlier analysis of the Sōka Gakkai:

devoting their energies wholeheartedly to whatever their occupation happened to be,[40] but some became Christians, some
ultra-rightists, some became Communists, some identified with
the Allies, and some joined one of the hundreds of newly arising religions.

The religious group which emerged as largest and most influential was the Sōka Gakkai. Thus, one explanation for the
success of the Sōka Gakkai (though not only of the Sōka
Gakkai) seems to be that it was a personal/group remedy for
the cultural value chaos in which Japanese found themselves
after the war, as the relative deprivation theory suggests. In
addition, the Sōka Gakkai also seems to fit some of the criteria
of the relative deprivation theory when viewed in relation to
the types of persons who are its members.

We saw in Chapter III that while the Sōka Gakkai media
projected an image of the "typical" Sōka Gakkai member as
being a happy and successful college-educated, young–middle-
aged male in a professional occupation, the several surveys we
reviewed led us to conclude that typical members were, rather,
of low (but not the lowest) socioeconomic status, their educational attainments and incomes were low, and they were
generally in labor, artisan, or small shop occupations. According
to various attitudinal measures, while Sōka Gakkai members
were no "worse" than ordinary Japanese on many items, on
none were they "better," and on some they were decidedly less
satisfactory. The Sōka Gakkai did seem to appeal to the alienated elements of Japanese urban society, and though it may
not have worsened or exploited them, it did not seem to have
cured them of their alienation in any dramatic way.

3. *The socializing function of the Sōka Gakkai.* This apparent similarity of the attitudes of Sōka Gakkai members to
those of ordinary Japanese deserves our closer attention. We
saw above that religious research in the West indicates that
members of sects are from the alienated lower and middle classes

---

James Allen Dator, "The Soka Gakkai—a Socio-Political Analysis,"
Contemporary Religions in Japan, VI (September, 1965), 205–42.

[40] See our evidence in Dator, " 'Protestant Ethic' in Japan," especially
pp. 35–37.

and that members of cults are from the relatively better-adjusted upper-middle and upper classes. The value profiles of cult members should thus be more like those of the general population than are those of sect members. If the Sōka Gakkai is a cult, it should not be surprising that the attitudes of Sōka Gakkai members are relatively similar to those of ordinary Japanese. Yet, we have suggested that the Sōka Gakkai is not a pure cult, but is instead a sect-cult. We made this distinction primarily because the demographic characteristics of Sōka Gakkai members were more like those of sectarians. How can we explain this apparent contradiction?

An explanation might be found in the answer given by Benton Johnson to his own question, "Do Holiness sects socialize in dominant values?" [41] Holiness sects in America are composed of individuals who are lower-educated, lower-status, alienated, and so forth. To many persons, Holiness sects seem to be no more than congregations of social outcasts—religious fanatics who, because they are outcasts, condemn all the pomp and vainglory of this wicked world. Yet Johnson suggests— convincingly, we believe—that actually the Holiness sects serve a significant pattern-maintenance function for society by socializing these marginal persons into dominant societal values.[42]

---

[41] Benton Johnson, "Do Holiness Sects Socialize in Dominant Values?" *Social Forces*, XXXIX (May, 1961), 307–17. See also Bernard Barber, "Acculturation and Messianic Movements," *American Sociological Review*, VI (October, 1941), 663–67; Leonard Cain, Jr., "Japanese-American Protestants: Acculturation and Assimilation," *Review of Religious Research*, III (1962), 113–21; Val Clear, "The Church of God: A Study in Social Adaptation," *Review of Religious Research*, II (Winter, 1961), 129–33; Russell Dynes, "Rurality, Migration, and Sectarianism," *Rural Sociology*, XXI (1956), 25–28; John Holt, "Holiness Religions: Cultural Shock and Social Reorganization," *American Sociological Review*, V (October, 1940), 740–47; Allen and Mary Spitzer, "Religious Reorganization Among the Montana Blackfeet," *Review of Religious Research*, II (1960), 19–35; J. Milton Yinger, "Religion and Social Change: Functions and Dysfunctions of Sects and Cults Among the Disprivileged," *Review of Religious Research*, IV (1963), 65–83; Frank Young, "Adaptation and Pattern Integration of a California Sect," *Review of Religious Research*, I (1960), 137–49.

[42] "These differences [between Holiness sects and upper- and middle-class Protestant denominations] should not be allowed to obscure the more fundamental fact of similarity of basic value orientation between

It is our suggestion that the Sōka Gakkai does the same for Japan and Japanese members. Whether it does so for America and American members is more debatable, but because the American members perceive the Sōka Gakkai as they would a fundamentalistic Christian sect and seem to define problems (e.g., drinking and sex) and their solution in ways identical with those of many American sectarian members, we feel the Sōka Gakkai can be said to perform the same function in America as well. Thus, in both societies, the Sōka Gakkai socializes marginal persons into dominant values.[43]

We are tempted to dwell on this point longer because it implies an underlying similarity of Japanese and American cultural values. But we will simply say that, indeed, we do feel this is the case, and we have tried to show elsewhere that it is the cluster of values generally designated the "Protestant Ethic" (the positive value of hard work, diligence, achievement, worldly success, self-improvement, etc.) that is found to be central in both countries.[44] The interesting thing here is that according to Johnson these are precisely the values into which the Holiness sects socialize their members.[45] We are strongly persuaded that this is also the case of the Sōka Gakkai in Japan.

Holiness groups and the more privileged classes. . . . Many of the strikingly different features of the Holiness groups probably function as mechanisms of socialization. There is evidence that the values in which Holiness adherents are socialized are similar to the dominant, institutionalized values of the larger society." Johnson, "Holiness Sects," p. 309.

[43] We are implying a three-fold typology of religio-ideological groups, based on their relation to the existing social order: some (mainly the churches and denominations) support, and encourage their members to support, the existing order; others (cults and some sects) socialize outcasts into the values of the dominant society; and the remainder (sects and some cults) encourage their members either to remain aloof from the world and await the divine (or natural) establishment of a new order, or else actually to subvert the existing order.

For examples of sects of this type, and to see further why we stress the belief that the Sōka Gakkai is closer to a cult like Christian Science than a sect like Jehovah's Witnesses, see Werner Cohn, "Jehovah's Witnesses as a Proletarian Movement," *American Scholar*, XXIV (Summer, 1955), 281–98, and Joseph Bram, "Jehovah's Witnesses and the Values of American Culture," *Transactions of the New York Academy of Science*, XIX (1956), 47–54.

[44] See my " 'Protestant Ethic' in Japan."

[45] Johnson, "Holiness Sects," pp. 310–17.

The Sōka Gakkai socializes its members into values similar to those of the Protestant Ethic.[46]

We conclude then that the social and personal function of the Sōka Gakkai in Japan and in the United States alike can be understood by reference to the relative deprivation theory on the one hand and its dominant value socializing activities on the other. The Sōka Gakkai (along with other cult-sectarian, religio-ideological groups, we keep pointing out) appeals to anomic or alienated persons and tries to infuse meaning into their lives through the inculcation of values that are essentially the same dominant values of both Japanese and American culture.

The Appeals of the Sōka Gakkai

In this narrative we have stressed the fact that in both Japan and the United States, the Sōka Gakkai is only one among many religio-ideological groups which perform this function. Its successful conversion of Americans can be said to be due primarily to coincidence. We discovered that almost all of the Americans were lower-class, poorly educated, alienated American servicemen who—most importantly—were married to Japanese female members of the Sōka Gakkai who were older than their husbands. We doubt that the Sōka Gakkai will spread much beyond people like these, at least for the time being, because of its Japanese culture-bound forms, language, and administration.

Its success in Japan can also be attributed in large measure to

---

[46] We stressed in our article above that the "Protestant Ethic" in Japan has nothing to do with Protestantism itself, of course, but primarily with a Japanese analogue adapted from Confucian ethics. Moreover we should add that we are not alone in making this observation. Both the Japan Socialist Party and the Japan Communist Party criticize the Sōka Gakkai precisely on this point, saying that the Sōka Gakkai is nothing but a paternalistic cover for capitalistic exploitation of the masses. Liston Pope pointed out in his famous book, *Millhands and Preachers* (New Haven, Conn.: Yale University Press, 1942), p. 29, *passim*, that the millowners encouraged the sects (primarily Holiness sects) because they pacified the millhands, stopped their drinking, and encouraged them to be regular and diligent workers.

coincidence. But if we were to seek for more comprehensive reasons why the Sōka Gakkai has been more successful than other groups in Japan, our answer would run along the following lines.

1. The Sōka Gakkai offers a simple but complete explanation of the entire world. For every possible question, the Sōka Gakkai has a definite, easy-to-understand answer. There is no ambiguity. For people who are bewildered by the complex modern world, the Sōka Gakkai provides an all-embracing explanation. Moreover, this explanation is presented as being highly scientific and very philosophical. Thus, especially members who do not have much formal higher education can be assured that their beliefs are very modern and very profound.

2. The Sōka Gakkai offers a Japanese explanation of the world. The Sōka Gakkai, unlike Christianity, or even orthodox Buddhism in Japan, is not an "imported Religion." Thus, although the Sōka Gakkai acknowledges that Nichiren Shōshū is a branch of Buddhism, it rejects the idea that the ultimate Buddha was Sakyamuni, who, they say, predicted that his powers would wane and that a new Buddha would arise. Hence, the true Buddha of our present age is none other than Nichiren himself, says the Sōka Gakkai, and he was, fortunately, a Japanese.

Of course, the Sōka Gakkai is not merely a Japanese nationalist religious group. It is internationalist in aspiration. A great deal of time and effort is being made to convert foreigners, and considerable energy is devoted to overseas missions. One of the Sōka Gakkai's proudest slogans is "world brotherhood," and it aims at the conversion of the world, not just of Japan. Nonetheless, the Sōka Gakkai quite consciously uses traditional Japanese symbols, such as the Rising Sun, the Japanese fan, and Mount Fuji, and its songs emphasize the theme that "with Japan as the base, we shall throw a bridge to every nation on earth." Also, Sōka Gakkai leaders frequently exhort the members to missionary activity because, since the Japanese are an advanced people with the true religion, they must assume the responsibility for saving the world. Unfortunately for the spread of "true religion," some of the Sōka Gakkai's critics find in its missionary enthusiasm much which reminds them of the Greater East Asian Co-Prosperity Sphere.[47]

In any event, the Sōka Gakkai seems to owe part of its success in Japan to its ability to satisfy the natural feelings of national superiority of the Japanese. To have been defeated in war, and yet actually to be a chosen people responsible for the spread of true religion, must be a source of considerable satisfaction.

3. The Sōka Gakkai is not a "new" religion. While its phenomenal growth is postwar, and while its organizational beginning was just before the war, still it claims to be no more than a lay organization affiliated with the seven hundred year old Nichiren Buddhism. The Sōka Gakkai's source, then, is not an old lady, or a milkman, or some other person of dubious divinity, as is the case for many of the "new" religions; it is the mighty Nichiren himself. That the Sōka Gakkai is both traditional and modern would seem to be a fact of no small significance. It is a modern organizational interpretation of a traditional Japanese faith.

4. The Sōka Gakkai is practical and "this-worldly." The true purpose of religion, says the Sōka Gakkai, is to give each person immediate, worldly, personal happiness. To tell people to be patient and do nothing but await some future or heavenly happiness, or that since all are "sinners," nothing can be done, is the way of religion which cannot produce results because it is false, they claim.

[47] The Korean Home Ministry, for example, took action against the Sōka Gakkai in Korea on the grounds that it was "against the basic policy of the Government, was undemocratic and antinationalistic" (*Japan Times*, December 20, 1964). The Sōka Gakkai appealed this as being a violation of Article Ten of the Korean Constitution, which guarantees freedom of religion. The claim of the Sōka Gakkai was upheld by the Seoul Appellate Court (*Japan Times*, March 4, 1965). However, the Home Ministry again proceeded against the Sōka Gakkai (and also another Japanese religious group, Tenrikyō), alleging that "the two religious groups had been resorting to intimidation and fraud in their attempts to disseminate their teaching" (*Japan Times*, August 6, 1965). Later, a group of South Korean college students were reported to have ransacked the Sōka Gakkai's headquarters in Seoul (*The Yomiuri*, August 21, 1965).

The Sōka Gakkai has also been outlawed in Nationalist China (*Japan Times*, March 21, 1966).

And yet the Sōka Gakkai insists that mere personal happiness is not enough. It is a contradiction to assume that the individual can be truly happy if the condition of society is unsatisfactory or chaotic. Personal happiness in such a situation is either illusory or selfish. Thus society must be perfected also. By the same token, it is not enough for one nation to be saved; all the world must be made happy as well. These claims of immediate satisfaction of personal and societal needs, especially when they are accompanied with the actual realization of many of the claims—as they so often appear to be—surely has appeal to persons dissatisfied with their current status in life.

At the same time, the Sōka Gakkai does not have a rigid or unusually lofty moral code. It does not require a radical rejection of "this world" and the adoption of an antisocietal ethic, as many Christian sects do. Of course, if a person is a drunkard, an uncontrollable gambler, a sexual profligate, or the like, he cannot expect to be happy, and thus these excesses must be avoided. But the Sōka Gakkai does not prohibit drinking, gambling, or sex. Rather, it suggests a common-sense, "golden mean" morality which is easily within the reach of a well-adjusted person, and it is precisely this "good adjustment" to life that the Sōka Gakkai seeks to effect.[48]

However, just as the Sōka Gakkai can hardly be called ascetic in its morals, neither can it be called contemplative. While daily prayers and occasional pilgrimages to Taisekiji are expected of believers, the prayers are generally of a repetitive nature, and while memorizing the Lotus Sutra may take some time, it and the other prayers are relatively uncomplicated and mesmerizing. Moreover, trips to Taisekiji can scarcely be called exercises in asceticism. There is no more hardship involved than there is in any trip in Japan, and the effervescent group spirit which per-

[48] It may appear that this emphasis upon "adjustment" is similar to the "acceptance of one's station in life" which would lead to quietism or withdrawal from the world. But such is not the case. The Sōka Gakkai, somewhat in the manner of Calvinistic Christianity, encourages a believer to be a successful, functioning member of the society in which he finds himself. In twentieth-century Japan, this is a paternalistic form of capitalism. Thus, Sōka Gakkai members are encouraged to be the "best of whatever you are and can be," not merely "content with whatever you are."

vades the sojourn must be a source of considerable satisfaction to most members.

5. While the Sōka Gakkai stresses the equality of all members in that all are equal when they enter the Sōka Gakkai, and social position is said to make no difference within the Sōka Gakkai (thus, we have been told, the janitor of a bank may be a teacher and the bank president his pupil), the Sōka Gakkai provides for intraorganizational ranking on the basis of individual effort. For example, it provides persons with such culturally honored titles as "Assistant Professor" or "Professor" or the like on the basis of objective tests covering the doctrine and practices of Nichiren Shōshū. Thus persons who did not have the opportunity to receive a higher education (and such is the case for most Sōka Gakkai members) are able to be "professors" within the Sōka Gakkai.

There are many other ranks as well which are positions of leadership within the various organizational subdivisions of the Sōka Gakkai. Many of the Japanese names chosen to designate both the groups and the ranks are similar to those used in the military. Partly for this reason the Sōka Gakkai is frequently alleged to be militaristic. While there are militaristic, or rather authoritarian, elements in the youth groups, we do not feel this is the case as far as the Sōka Gakkai as a whole is concerned. The flow chart depicting the organization of the Sōka Gakkai looks as much like that of a business as it does of a military organization, and the Sōka Gakkai is said to have quite consciously studied and adopted the most useful administrative structures and techniques of modern organizational theory when it made its structural reorganizations after the war.

But our suggestion about the ranks is that the primary function of ranking within the Sōka Gakkai is different from that of either a military or a business organization. In these latter organizations, the main function of ranks is to enable the higher to control the lower; it is to see that top-level staff decisions are carried out by the line operatives. While this of course is not absent from the Sōka Gakkai by any means, the main function of ranks within the Sōka Gakkai, from the individual member's point of view, seems to be to give status to persons whom society has generally overlooked. Thus these ranks have more of a sociopsychological function than a controlling or military one. Moreover, all ranks appear to be obtained on the basis of individual effort within the Sōka Gakkai rather than by seniority or social prestige. This of course sets the Sōka Gakkai off from most organizations in Japan, where individual effort often counts for little (indeed, it may be negatively evaluated), and age is so important.

The main activity which determines a member's rank is his effort to convert persons to the Sōka Gakkai. These conversion techniques, especially *shakubuku*, but also *shōju*, are very important in accounting for the success of the Sōka Gakkai, as well as for pointing out its greatest fault in the eyes of non-believers. As far as the Sōka Gakkai member himself is concerned, however, since *shakubuku* and *shōju* are major activities of the group; are the measure by which his merit as a member is evaluated; are activities which require him to behave in ways which are contrary to those of his normal interpersonal relations; and are frequently performed on strangers by a small group of members (thus, as an act of small-group solidarity, reinforcing him in the correctness of his activities), *shakubuku* is of as much importance to the individual as it is to the organization itself.

Our conclusion then is that the Sōka Gakkai should be conceptualized as a value-creating action group, precisely as its name signifies. While concern for personal morals and the worth of study and contemplation are by no means lacking, the focus of the Sōka Gakkai, as *shakubuku* makes especially clear, is primarily upon the creating of individual value through group action. The individual is caught in a web of activities which give rise to and reinforce his faith. Thus, the insistent "busyness" and the group nature of the activities interact to confirm the believer in his faith, and to discourage objective or negative evaluation of it.

Concluding Remarks

The Japanese do not seem to be a "religious" people. Less than 20 per cent of our Tokyo sample (and 35 per cent of a

1958 nationwide sample)[49] indicated that they were members of any religious group and only about one third believed in the existence of God. So few Japanese—even those who were members of any religious group—can be called religiously active, that a whole section of our questionnaire (fifty items) devoted to religious behavior and religious information proved to be of less value than we had hoped it would be. A religious behavior inventory we constructed (a composite of responses to separate items relating to attendance at religious services, saying prayers, contributing money to religious groups, listening to religious programs on television or radio, talking about religious problems with friends, and other religious activities) showed that on our eight-point scale, 42 per cent of our sample scored 0 (no religious activities), 24 per cent scored 1, and only 34 per cent scored 2 or more. Unlike the United States, where religious affiliation and belief in God are considered normative, the religious person—especially the deeply devout and religiously active person—in Japan is quite unusual. Indeed, it can be argued that active religious affiliation in Japan can be considered antisocial behavior. We are convinced from our six years' experience in Japan that the small group—primarily, for the male and unmarried female, the occupational group, and for the mother, her children—serves as a very effective surrogate for the religious faith of the Westerner.

Jirō Kamishima has stressed that individualism is possible in the West because the individual is never alone. He is always at least in a two-man group: God is with him. But this is not the case for the Japanese. Even for the religious, the solitary hermit is extremely rare.[50] The small group is God for most Japanese.

In finally evaluating the Sōka Gakkai, then, in spite of its size and fervor, its marginality within Japanese culture must be remembered. Earlier in this chapter we suggested that most Japanese seemed to have utilized complete identification toward and activity within their occupational groups as the basis for

---

[49] Sōichi Suetsuna *et al.*, *Nihon no Kokuminsei* (Tōkyō: Shiseidō, 1961), p. 181.

[50] Jirō Kamishima, *Nihonjin no Kekkonkan* (Tōkyō: Tsukuma Shōbō, 1964), chap. xxvi.

restructuring their values after the war. True, many turned to religion, but most did not. Thus, the committed religious affiliate, be he Sōka Gakkai, Christian, or something else, is an unusual man, indicating his inability to find satisfaction within his occupational group either because his occupational status and educational standards are too low to enable him to fulfill his ambitions within that group (as is the case for Sōka Gakkai members),[51] or because his status and educational achievements are too high to enable him to be satisfied by such occupational identification alone (as seems to be the case for the Christian).

This is certainly not to say that the Sōka Gakkai is unimportant. It is the largest group of any kind in Japan. It continues to move successfully into Japanese politics. It daily gains new members. It works eagerly to build the third civilization.

[51] See Dator, " 'Protestant Ethic' in Japan."

APPENDIX I

English-Language Tests Given by the Study Department to American Members of the Sōka Gakkai for Appointment as Lecturer or Associate-Assistant Professor

A. Given at Yokosuka, January, 1965. See also *Seikyo News*, January 26, 1965, p. 2. Model answers are given in the same issue.

   I. Give a brief explanation of the following terms:
      1. Jikkai
      2. Sandai-hiho
      3. Nikko Shonin
      4. Tenju Kyoju
      5. Shijo Kingo

   II. Combine A-block words with the suitable B-block words:

A Block	B Block
1. Tsunesaburo Makiguchi	1. Atsuhara Persecution
2. Sakyamuni	2. Hobo
3. Ti-en-tai the Great	3. Philosophy of Value
4. Jinshiro, Yagoro, Yarokuro	4. Makahikan
5. Goroso	5. Hokekyo

   III. Explain about "The Third Civilization."

   IV. Explain Sansho, or three proofs.

B. In the *Seikyo News*, August 10, 1965, p. 2. Model answers are given in the same issue.

      1. Answer the criticism that the Sokagakkai is a fascist group.
      2. Explain the principle of "Shiki-Shin Funi."
      3. Explain the following sentence: "When you advance in the practice and study of the True Buddhism, Sansho Shima (Three Obstacles and Four Devils) will befall you furiously."
      4. Explain briefly the following:
         A. Inga Guji

  B. Ichienbudai
  C. Rokuroso
  D. Myoyaku
  E. Shudatsu Sotai

C. In the *Seikyo Times*, January 21, 1966, p. 12. Model answers
are given in the same issue.

  For Assistant Lecturer

  1. Explain briefly the following Buddhist terms. (a)
     Mappo, (b) Myoyaku
  2. Describe briefly the following persons. (a) Raju
     Sanzo (Kumarajiva), (b) Abutsu-bo
  3. What is the meaning of Hendoku Iyaku?
  4. Write on Christianity from the viewpoint of the
     principle of Sansho.
  5. Explain Sansho Shima.
  6. What is the "spirit of Gokuyo"?

  For Lecturer

  1. Explain briefly the following Buddhist terms. (a)
     Hokekyo, (b) San-dai-hiho
  2. Describe briefly the following persons. (a) Nikkan
     Shonin, (b) Nanjo Tokimitsu
  3. What is the difference between Shoju and Shaku-
     buku?
  4. Explain the sentence, "Mujohoju Fugu-jitoku."
  5. Explain Sanrui-no-Goteki.
  6. Point out the errors in the assumption that religion
     and science are incompatible.

Written and oral tests like these are used to determine promotion within the Study Department of the Sōka Gakkai. The complete list of ranks, and the number of persons holding each rank
(Japanese and non-Japanese members apparently included) was
given by the *Seikyo Times*, February 1, 1966, p. 5, as follows:

Professors	519
Associate Professors	3,660
Assistant Professors	13,445
Assoc. Assist. Professors	81,261
Lecturers	284,670
Assistant Lecturers	789,882
	1,173,437

APPENDIX II

Thirty-Item "Traditionalism Scale," According to Its Seven Subcategories, Developed by Tajirō Hayasaka

(See Chapter III, Note 26)

SUPERIOR-INFERIOR RELATIONS

1. Even if it works to his own personal disadvantage, it is natural for a boss to protect a subordinate when the subordinate does something wrong.
2. It is desirable for a subordinate to be willing to go through fire and water for his boss.
3. It is natural for your boss to look out for you even after working hours.
4. Even if you think it is wrong, if a superior tells you to do something, you should do it without comment.

FAMILISM

5. As the focal point in the family, of course the oldest son should look after the family in the future.
6. It is desirable for a business firm to be like a family.
7. People like the head of a company or a foreman are just the same as the head of a family.
8. A young wife should obey the customs of her husband's household.

FILIAL PIETY

9. A person who does not follow filial piety is not an honorable man.
10. You should not contradict your parents even if what they say is impossible.
11. Nowadays, people don't know too much about parents' love (*on*).
12. If you want to marry someone your parents don't approve of, you had better give it up.
13. Since your parents have done so much for you when you were young, it is natural that you should take care of them when you grow up.

MAIN FAMILY-BRANCH FAMILY RELATIONS

14. All relatives should gather around and cooperate with the main family (*honke*).
15. Even if it's nearly impossible for the branch family (*bunke*), it should obey decisions of the main family.
16. Because the relationship between the main and branch family is one of the good things about Japan, we should carefully preserve it.
17. Members of the branch family should always show up for main family religious ceremonies and festivals.
18. It is natural for the main family to take care of the branch families.

HOMETOWN CONSCIOUSNESS

19. Because your seniors in your hometown have helped you in many ways, you must be deferential to them.
20. You should look after your juniors in your hometown.

DESIRE FOR HARMONY

21. It is best to conduct yourself just as everyone around you does.
22. Because your place of business should always be congenial, it is best not to express opinions which might cause disagreement.
23. Because it is bad if you don't help others, you should always repay any kindness shown you.
24. No matter how correct you think it is, it is best not to talk about things others will laugh at.

CONVENTIONAL CONDUCT

25. It is natural to return a gift with a gift.
26. It is natural to reward people who help you arrange your marriage, or aid you in getting a job.
27. You must not forget to be deferential to a family that rendered aid to your family in the past (for example, when your parents were young).
28. Even if people who helped you in the past are rude to you now, you must not bear a grudge against them.
29. You must be very gracious to people who have lent you land, a home, or money.
30. Even if it is sometimes inconvenient, it is best to go along with custom.

APPENDIX III

The Five Personality Scales Used in This Study

(See Chapter III, Note 27)

AUTHORITARIANISM[1]

1. There are two kinds of people in the world: the weak and the strong.
2. The most important thing to teach children is absolute obedience to their parents.
3. Prison is too good for sex criminals; they should be publicly whipped, or worse.
4. Any good leader should be strict with people under him in order to gain their respect.
5. No decent man would marry a woman who has had sexual relations before marriage.

ANOMIE[2]

1. There's little use writing to public officials because often they aren't really interested in the problems of the average man.
2. Nowadays a person has to live pretty much for today and let tomorrow take care of itself.
3. In spite of what some people say, the lot of the average man is getting worse, not better
4. It's hardly fair to bring children into the world with the way things look for the future.
5. These days a person doesn't really know whom he can count on.

---

[1] Adapted from Alan Roberts and Milton Rokeach, "Anomie, Authoritarianism and Prejudice," *American Journal of Sociology*, LXI (January, 1956), 357.
[2] *Ibid.*

FAITH-IN-PEOPLE[3]

1. You can trust people.
2. You can't be too careful in your dealings with people.
3. If you don't watch out, people will take advantage of you.
4. Most people are inclined to help others.
5. Most people don't care about other people, but only look out for themselves.

MISTRUST OF PUBLIC OFFICIALS[4]

1. People who go into public office are usually out for all they can get.
2. Elected officials become tools of special interests, no matter what.
3. Local officials soon lose touch with the people who elected them.
4. If people knew what was really going on in high places, it would blow the lid off things.

SENSE OF CITIZEN DUTY[5]

1. It isn't so important to vote when you know your party doesn't have a chance to win.
2. A good many local elections aren't important enough to bother with
3. So many people vote in the national elections that it doesn't matter much to me whether I vote or not.
4. If a person doesn't care how an election comes out, he shouldn't vote.
5. Politics and government seem so complicated that a person like me can't really understand what's going on.

[3] Adapted from Wayne Thompson and John Horton, "Political Alienation as a Force in Political Action," *Social Forces*, XXXVIII (March, 1960), 195.
[4] Source: John Horton and Wayne Thompson, "Powerlessness and Political Negativism," *American Journal of Sociology*, LXVII (March, 1962), 486.
[5] Source: Angus Campbell *et al.*, *The Voter Decides* (Evanston, Ill.: Row, Peterson, 1954), p. 197.

APPENDIX IV

Songs of the Sōka Gakkai

The following are English versions of songs sung by Japanese and foreign members of the Sōka Gakkai. The translations are not ours.

1. *Song of World Propagation (Sekai kōfu no uta)*[1]

   Behold! Vigorous spirits of youth are filling the world. To the snow-capped peaks of the Himalayas, and to the perpetual flow of the Hwang Ho, we all will go with lofty ideal. Ah, we are high-spirited in the mission of worldwide propagation.

2. *Songs of American Propagation (Amerika kōfu no uta)*[2]

   The time has come to spread the true enlightment. Now firmly we stand on this ground. America Kosen-rufu is in our hands.

   He who believes is always ready. Newly found youth is full of vigor. We will fight for America together with carrying the flag. America Kosen-rufu is in our hands.

   Though the rod be hard, nothing can dismay our strong zeal and enthusiasm. Refute the wrong religions and let's go. We look toward Mt. Fuji. America Kosen-rufu is in our hands.

3. *Song of Conversion (Kakushin no uta)*[3]

   With the strength of a flood we will spread the law throughout the world. Newly found youth will bring a storm of criticism. The light of the Gohonzon will pierce the clouds of ignorance.

---

[1] *Seikyo News,* July 14, 1964.
[2] *Ibid.,* January 14, 1964.
[3] *Ibid.*

Daily striving toward Kosen-rufu will bring the strength of the Universe to strike the alien. Newly found youth will bring enlightenment to the world.

Spiritual things alone do not make people happy. Neither do material things make people happy. Only the spread of the True Buddhism will bring happiness. The bell of peace will ring when the philosophy is established.

4. A Song for Victory (Shōri e no uta)[4]

Now is the time for revolution. Indestructible philosophy upheld, great advancement of youths which shake the Earth overcomes devils and obstacles.

5. Footsteps of Progress (Zenshin no ashi-oto)[5]

Let our footsteps of progress sound loud, youth filled with vigor and power, as the new idealistic age is coming. Let us stride the path with pride of pioneers.

Let the cry of reformation echo, youth filled with wisdom and courage, as the leader of the world now stands grandly. Let us establish the great Buddhist democracy.

6. Song for a New Age (Shin-seiki no uta)[6]

Noble and bold are young eagles in flight through heaven's arch unfurled.

Firm is our trust in our leader's might—pillar of the world!

For our brothers in misery, let us strive anew.

Save them all, through our faith, merciful and true!

Where plays the dolphin wild and free resounds our leader's command

Over the face of the seven seas, forth to every land.

Know our firm and steadfast faith makes the whole world one.

March along—now's the time! We have but begun.

When e'er the lion raises his voice, even the earth trembles too.

So shall it be as we answer the call: Kosen-rufu!

With the sword of truth and power, banish evil's sway.

Built on faith, it is our newly dawning day.

[4] *Ibid.*, December 15, 1964.
[5] *Ibid.*, August 4, 1964.
[6] *Seikyo Times*, August, 1965, p. 30.

BIBLIOGRAPHY

Sōka Gakkai Publications

THERE IS NO SHORTAGE of publications by the Sōka Gakkai about its activities, and all of the items listed below should be able to be purchased by writing the Seikyo Press, 18–29 Shinanomachi, Shinjuku-ku, Tokyo, Japan, or to the Sōka Gakkai Los Angeles Kaikan, 2102 East First Street, Los Angeles, California 90033.

The basic writings of Nichiren are found in his Gosho, the Sōka Gakkai's multivolume edition of which was first published in 1952. An English translation is said to be in preparation. The political philosophy of Nichiren finds its major expression in his *Risshō Ankoku Ron*. Tsunesaburō Makiguchi's major work, *Kachiron*, is also available in English as *The Philosophy of Value*. While Josei Toda's speeches are collected in a multi-volume Japanese edition, there does not seem to be an English counterpart, but many of Daisaku Ikeda's speeches are available in English: *Lectures on Buddhism* (3 vols.), *Guidance Memo, Science and Religion, The Human Revolution* (3 vols.), and *The Complete Works of Daisaku Ikeda* (1 vol. so far).

The political party of the Soka Gakkai, the Kōmeitō, has published a number of statements of its policy. A recent convenient statement, in Japanese, is *Taishū Kōfuku o Mezashite: Kōmeitō no Seisaku* (2 vols.).

Among other English-language publications are the "This Is the Soka Gakkai" series, *Lecture on the Sutra*, and *The Nichiren Shoshu Sokagakkai*. English-language periodicals include the weekly magazine, *Seikyo Times*, which replaced the newspaper, *Seikyo News*, and the *World Tribune*.

Following are some of the major Japanese-language periodicals published by the Sōka Gakkai:*

Kachi Kōzō, begun by Makiguchi in 1942 and published for five numbers before being suppressed by the government.

---

* We have found that statements in the Japanese-language publications are more likely to be reliable than are those in the English-language publications.

Daibyaku Renge, a monthly instructional magazine, begun in 1949.

Seikyō Shimbun, a daily newspaper, begun in 1951.

Seikyō Graphic, a weekly pictorial magazine with some English captions and commentary, begun in 1959.

Daisan Bunmei, a monthly journal published by the Student Division since 1960.

Ushio, a monthly political journal originally published by the Political Division in 1960, now sold widely at Japanese newsstands as a major intellectual journal dealing with social, economic, and political matters.

Zenshin, a monthly instructional magazine for leaders.

Tōyō Gakujutsu Kenkyū, a monthly academic journal published by the Institute of Oriental Philosophy since 1964.

Shūkan Genron, published weekly by the Linguistics Division since 1962.

Tōdai, a monthly journal published by the Education Division since 1962.

Kibō no Tomo, published monthly for the Youth Division since 1964.

Kibō Life, a monthly magazine for upper primary and junior high school children.

Kibō Ehon, a monthly magazine for lower primary and kindergarten children.

Shō-Chū Gakusei Bunka Shimbun, a daily newspaper for elementary and junior high school children.

Gakuen Journal, a weekly magazine for university students.

Seinen Journal, a weekly magazine for young men, begun in 1967.

Kayo Journal, a weekly magazine for young women, begun in 1967.

In addition to many pamphlets and policy statements, the political party, Kōmeitō, publishes a daily newspaper, *Kōmei Shimbun,* and a monthly political journal, *Kōmei,* both started in 1962, and *Kōmei Graphic,* a weekly pictorial magazine, started in 1967.

Selected English-Language Publications about the Sōka Gakkai

Azumi, Koya. "Social Basis of a New Religious Party: The Komeito of Japan." Mimeographed copy of a paper read before the Annual Meeting of the American Sociological Association, August, 1967

Bloom, Alfred. "Observations in the Study of Contemporary Nichiren Buddhism," *Contemporary Religions in Japan*, VI (March, 1965), 58–74.

Brannen, Noah. "A Visit to the Soka Gakkai Headquarters," *Contemporary Religions in Japan*, II (March, 1961), 55–62.

——. "A Visit to Taisekiji, Head Temple of the Soka Gakkai," *Contemporary Religions in Japan*, II (June, 1961), 13–30.

——. "False Religions, Forced Conversions, Iconoclasm," *Contemporary Religions in Japan*, V (September, 1964), 232–52.

——. "The Soka Gakkai's Theory of Value," *Contemporary Religions in Japan*, V (June, 1964), 143–54.

——. "The Teachings of the Soka Gakkai," *Contemporary Religions in Japan*, III (September, 1962), 247–63.

Dator, James Allen. "The Soka Gakkai: A Socio-Political Interpretation," *Contemporary Religions in Japan*, VII (September, 1965), 205–42.

——. "The Soka Gakkai in Japanese Politics," *A Journal of Church and State*, IX (Spring, 1967), 211–37.

Dugliss, Roderick B. "The Komeito and the Japanese Elections," *Economic and Political Weekly* (India), February 11, 1967, pp. 377–81.

——. "The Foreign Policy of the *Komeito*." Pp. 845–66 in *The Final Report of the Ford Research Project*. Tokyo: International Christian University, 1967.

Flagler, J. M. "A Chanting in Japan," *The New Yorker*, November 16, 1966.

Helton, William. "Political Prospects of the Soka Gakkai," *Pacific Affairs*, XXXVIII (Fall–Winter, 1965–66), 231–44.

Kudo, Takaya. "The Faith of the Soka Gakkai," *Contemporary Religions in Japan*, II (June, 1961), 1–12.

Kumasaka, Y. "Soka Gakkai: Group Psychologic Study of a New Religio-Political Organization," *American Journal of Psychotherapy*, XX (July, 1966), 462–70.

McCrimmon, Mary. "From Christianity to Soka Gakkai," *The Japan Missionary Bulletin*, XVIII (July, 1964), 397–402.

Moos, Felix. "Religion and Politics in Japan: The Case of the Soka Gakkai," *Asian Survey*, III (March, 1963), 136–42.

Murata, Kiyoaki. "Soka Gakkai," *Hemisphere*, X (May, 1966), 8–12.

Offner, Clark, and Henry Van Straelen. *Modern Japanese Religion*. New York: Twayne Publishers, 1963. Pp. 98–109 deal with the Sōka Gakkai.

Okamoto, Richard. "A New Faith Called Soka Gakkai Raises Old

Problems in Modern Japan," *Look*, September 10, 1963, pp. 15–26.

Morris, Ivan. "Soka Gakkai Brings 'Absolute Happiness,'" *New York Times Magazine*, July 18, 1965.

Olson, Lawrence. "The Value Creation Society, Soka Gakkai: A Japanese Religious and Political Phenomenon," *American Universities Field Staff Reports*, East Asia Series, X, No. 6 (Japan), June, 1964.

Ramseyer, Robert. "The Soka Gakkai," in *Studies in Japanese Culture*, No. 1. (University of Michigan Center for Japanese Studies, Occasional Paper 9, 1965.)

————. "The Soka Gakkai and the Japanese Local Elections of 1963," *Contemporary Religions in Japan*, IV (December, 1963), 287–303.

Saito, Ken. "Soka Gakkai: Third Force in Japanese Politics?" *Orient/West*, VII, 1962.

Sheldon, Charles. "Religion and Politics in Japan: The Soka Gakkai," *Pacific Affairs*, XXXIII, (December, 1960), 382–86.

"Soka Gakkai and the Nichiren Sho Sect," *Contemporary Religions in Japan*, I (March, 1960), 55–70, (June, 1960), 48–54.

Thomsen, Harry. *The New Religions of Japan*. Rutland, Vt.: Charles E. Tuttle, 1963. Pp. 81–108 deal with the Sōka Gakkai.

White, James. "Mass Movements and Democracy: Sokagakkai in Japanese Politics," *American Political Science Review*, LXI (September, 1967), 744–50.

Selected Japanese-Language Publications about the Sōka Gakkai

Akiya, Josei (ed.). *Sōka Gakkai no Riron to Jissen*. Tōkyō: Hōshōin, 1964.

Burando Kabushiki Kaisha and Ichiba Chōsa Kenkyūjo. *Seikyō Brand Research*. Tokyo: Mimeographed, October, 1964.

Higashi Honganji Shūkyō Kenkyūjo. *Sōka Gakkai no Kentō*. Kyōto: Hyakken, 1962.

Fujiwara, Hirotatsu. "Sōka Gakkai Shin Nana-nen Keikaku no Shinri," *Toki*, July, 1964, pp. 176–80.

Hayasaka, Tajirō. *Shinkō Shūkyō ni Kansuru Shakai Shinrigaku-teki Kenkyū*. Tōkyō: Mimeographed at Rikkyō University, 1965.

Ichikawa, Masahiro. "Sōka Gakkai wa Fashizumu de wa nai," *Gendai no Me*, December, 1964, pp. 149–55.

Ichiyanagi, Toichirō. "Kitai o Uragitta Hoshu to Kakushin," *Jiyū*, August, 1965, pp. 58–67.

Ikado, Fujio. "Shinkō Shūkyō no Dōkō to Kadai," *Jiyū*, July, 1964, pp. 128–39.

———. "Shinkō Shūkyō no Sōshiki to Sono Shakai-teki Kinō," *Seishōnen Mondai*, December, 1962, pp. 6–13.

Ishida, Ikuo. "Kōmeitō to 'Shōmin Seiji,'" *Gendai no Riron*, February, 1965, pp. 50–59.

———. "Nihonteki Genjitsu no Ichi Danmen: Sōka Gakkai," *Gendai no Riron*, March, 1965, pp. 2–22.

———. "Shakubuku no Uchimaku," *Gendai no Me*, September, 1964, pp. 85–93.

———. *Sōka Gakkai*. Tōkyō: Sanitchi Shōten, 1965.

Ishikawa, Taidō. *Shakubuku no Shakubuku*. Tōykō: Nihonbushō Kankōkai, 1957.

———. "Sōka Gakkai wa Henshitsu Shita ka?" *Daihōrin*, February, 1964, pp. 126–30.

———. *Zoku Shakubuku no Shakubuku*. Tōkyō: Nihonbushō Kankōkai, 1962.

Itō, Yoshitaka. *Sōka Gakkai no Hihan*. Tōkyō: Shinshū Gakuryō, 1962.

Kasahara, Kazuo. *Seiji to Shūkyō*. Tōkyō: Asoka Shuppansha, 1965.

———. "Sōka Gakkai ga Nerau-mono," *Daihōrin*, August, 1964, pp. 38–61.

———. *Tenkanki no Shūkyō*. Tōkyō: Nippon Hōsō Shuppan Kyōkai, 1966.

Katsube, Gen. "60-Nendai no Shin Fashizumu," *Gendai no Me*, September, 1964, pp. 54–64.

Kodaira, Yoshihei. *Sōka Gakkai*. Tōkyō: Hoshoin, 1962.

"Kōmeitō wa Nani o Nerau Ka?" *Gendai no Me*, April, 1965, pp. 40–71.

Maruyama, Kunio. "Ikeda Kaichō e no Muttsu no Shitsumon," *Gendai no Me*, September, 1964, pp. 72–82.

Masujima, Hiroshi. "Seiji Shinshutsu no Imi to Haikei," *Gendai no Me*, September, 1964, pp. 42–53.

Miki, Jun. *Shashin Sōka Gakkai*. Tōkyō: Kawade Shōbō, 1968.

Miyata, Mitsuo. "Shūkyō Seitō to Minshushugi," *Sekai*, May, 1965.

Mochida, Yukio. "Kōmeitō no Yakushin to Kabe," *Jiyū*, August, 1965, pp. 68–76.

Moriyama, Satoru. *Sōka Gakkai no Machigai o Tadsu*. Tōkyō: Nippon Iesu Kirisuto Kyōdan Tōkyō Shuppanbu, 1963.

Murakami, Shigeyoshi. "Seiji Shinshutsu no Haikei to Nihonteki Jōkyō," *Gendai no Me*, April, 1965, pp. 40–49.

———. "Shūkyō no Handoka to Seiji Riyō," *Gendai no Me*, June, 1963, pp. 85–93.

———. "Sōka Gakkai no Seiji Shinshutsu," *Nihonshi Kenkyū*, 1962, pp. 71–74.

———. "Sōka Gakkai no Shakaiteki Yakuwari wa Nanika?" *Ronsō*, September, 1962, pp. 74–84.

———. *Sōka Gakkai to Kōmeitō*. Tōkyō: Nihon Bunkasha, 1965.

Muramatsu, Takeshi. "Nihon no Kindaika to Nichirenshū," *Chūō Kōron*, March, 1965, pp. 48–62.

Murata, Kiyoaki. "Seiji to Shūkyō wa Ryōritsu Subeki Ka?" *Keizai Orai*, August, 1964, pp. 67–75.

Nichirenshū Shūmuin Kyōmubu. *Sōka Gakkai Hihan*. Tōkyō: Nichirenshū Shuppanbu, 1955.

Nishijima, Hisashi. *Kōmeitō*. Tōkyō: Sekkasha, 1968.

Oda, Makoto. "Dai-san no Michi wa Izuko e?" *Toki*, September, 1964, pp. 116–29.

Okasaka, Tarō. "Hajimatte iru San-in Senkyo," *Bungei Shunju*, July, 1964, pp. 88–92.

Ōzawa, Nobuo. "Sōka Gakkai, Kono Rinjin-tachi," *Tembō*, June, 1965, pp. 164–79.

Sakamoto, Mamoru. "Sōka Gakkai to Kōmeitō," *Jiyū*, October, 1964, pp. 74–83.

Saki, Akio. " 'Daisan Bunmei' no Gen-ei," *Bunka Hyōron*, June, 1963, pp. 2–11.

———. "Kōmeitō no Seisaku o Hihan suru," *Zen-ei*, July, 1965, pp. 199–211.

———. "Kōmeitō no Seisaku to Honshitsuron," *Ekonomisuto*, July 27, 1965.

———. "Saishingata Shūkyō, Sōka Gakkai no Kaibō," *Daihōrin*, September, 1957, pp. 40–52.

———. "Sensō Suru Sōka Gakkai," *Daihōrin*, October, 1957, pp. 80–91.

———. "Shinkō Shūkyō no Jitsugen to Mondaiten," *Toshi Mondai*, October, 1959, pp. 17–25.

———. "Shūkyō Dantai to Seiji Katsudō," *Hyōron Bunka*, September, 1962, pp. 12–19.

———. "Shūkyō ni Kansuru Komponteki na Taidō ni Tsuite," *Zen-ei*, May, 1963, pp. 46–55.

———. "Sōka Gakkai no Seiji Rosen," *Zen-ei*, February, 1963, pp. 54–62.

————, et al. "Chōsen Suru Daisan Bunmei," Gendai no Me, September, 1964, pp. 94–105.

Sekai Bukkyō Kyōkai. Sōka Gakkai o Shakubuku Suru. Tōkyō: Sekai Bukkyō Kyōkai, 1962.

"Shinkyō no Jiyū to Seiji Katsudō no Jiyū," Zen-ei, May, 1963, pp. 94–101.

Shiobara, Tsutome. "Sōka Gakkai Ideorogi," Tembō, June, 1965, pp. 34–57.

"Sōka Gakkai no 'Seiji Shinshutsu,' " Shakaitō, July, 1964, pp. 160–63.

Suzuki, Hiroshi. "Toshi Kasō no Shūkyō Shūdan," Shakaigaku Kenkyū (Tōhoku University), 1963, pp. 81–102, and 1964, pp. 50–90.

Suzuki, Shizuo. "Sōka Gakkai to Chihō Senkyo," Zen-ei, September, 1963, pp. 106–19.

Taguchi, Kuji. "Rinen to Seisaku no Mujun," Gendai no Me, April, 1965, pp. 50–57.

Takagi, Hirō. "Kōmeitō Shinshutsu," Keisai Zemina-, February, 1965, pp. 28–32.

————, et al. "Shūkyō, Fashizumu, Demokrashii," Gendai no Me, April, 1965, pp. 58–71.

Takase, Hiroi. Daisan Bunmei no Shūkyo. Tōkyō: Kōbundō, 1962.

————. Kōmeitō. Tōkyō: Gakushu Kenkyūsha, 1964.

Tanaka, Nikkō. Nichiren Shōshū Sōka Gakkai Hashaku Hayawakari 12 Mondōshū. Tōkyō: Dairoku Kōtsuku Kyōiku Iinkai, 1955.

Takahashi, Tomomichi. Sōka Gakkai ga Shinjitsu Nara. Tōkyō: Shinjinsha, 1959.

Togawa, Isamu. "Chihō Senkyo no Kagi Nigiru Sōka Gakkai," Toki, May, 1963, pp. 70–74.

Tōkyō Daigaku Shakai Gakka and Tōkyō Joshi Daigaku Shaki Gakka. Sōka Gakkai. Tokyo: University of Tokyo Department of Sociology, 1963.

Tominaga, Heisaku. "Bōryoku Shūkyō to Iwareru Sōka Gankai no Shōtai," Daihōrin, March, 1956, pp. 71–75.

Tsunoda, Shizaburō. "Sōka Gakkai to Wareware," Seiki, September, 1963.

————. "Sōka Gakkai: Sono Eikō to Hisan," Seiki, February, 1963, pp. 40–50.

Tsuji, Takehisa. "Kōmeitō no Kihon Seisaku," Ekonomisuto, September 7, 1965.

Tsukamoto, Tetsu. "Shinkō Shūkyō no Shakaiteki Eikyō," Kyōiku to Igaku, November, 1959, pp. 13–18.

Tsurumi, Shunsuke, *et al. Shakubuku.* Tōkyō: Sanhō, 1963.
Umehara, Takeshi. "Sōka Gakkai no Tetsugaku-teki, Shūkyō-teki Hihan," *Shisō no Kagaku,* December, 1964, pp. 83–95.
Watanabe, Baiyu. "Sūji Kara Mita Shin Shūkyō," *Daihōrin,* March, 1964, pp. 100–6.

Selected Works on Japanese Religion and Culture*

Abegglen, James C. "Subordination and Autonomy Attitudes of Japanese Workers," *American Journal of Sociology,* LXIII (1957), 181–89.
Anesaki, Masaharu. *History of Japanese Religion.* Rutland, Vt: Charles Tuttle, 1963.
———. *Nichiren: The Buddhist Prophet.* London: Oxford University Press, 1949.
———. *The Religious Life of the Japanese People.* Tokyo: Kokusai Bunka Shinkokai, 1961.
Basabe, Fernando M. *Japanese Youth Confronts Religion: A Sociological Survey.* Tokyo: Sophia University in cooperation with Charles Tuttle, 1967.
Bellah, Robert (ed.). *Religion and Progress in Modern Asia.* New York: Free Press of Glencoe, 1965.
———. "Religious Aspects of Modernization in Turkey and Japan," *American Journal of Sociology,* LXIV (July, 1958), 1–5.
———. *Tokugawa Religion—The Values of Pre-Industrial Japan.* Glencoe, Ill.: Free Press, 1957.
Dator, James Allen. "The Life History and Attitudes of Japanese High Court Judges," *Western Political Quarterly,* XX (June, 1967), 408–39.
———. "The 'Protestant Ethic' in Japan," *Journal of Developing Areas,* I (October, 1966), 23–40.
Hall, John W., *et al. Twelve Doors to Japan.* New York: McGraw-Hill, 1965.
Hall, Robert. *Shūshin: The Ethics of a Defeated Nation.* New York: Columbia University Press, 1949.
Hammer, Raymond. *Japan's Religious Ferment.* London: SCM Press, 1961.
Hayashi, Chikio, *et al. Zusetsu Nihonjin no Kokuminsei.* Tōkyō: Shiseidō, 1965.

* All issues of the journal, *Contemporary Religions in Japan,* should also be consulted.

Kitagawa, Joseph. *Religion in Japanese History*. New York: Columbia University Press, 1966.

McFarland, H. Neill. *The Rush Hour of the Gods: A Study of New Religious Movements in Japan*. New York: Macmillan, 1967.

Muramatsu, Tsuneo, *et al. Nihonjin*. Tōkyō: Reimei Shōbō, 1963.

Nagasawa, Masao. *Zusetsu Nihonjin no Seikatsu*. Tōkyō: Shiseidō, 1965.

Nivison, David, and Arthur Wright (eds.). *Confucianism in Action*. Stanford, Calif.: Stanford University Press, 1959.

Plath, David. "The Fate of Utopia: Adaptive Tactics in Four Japanese Groups," *American Anthropologist*, LXVIII (October, 1966), 1152–62.

———. "Utopian Rhetoric: Conversion and Conversation in a Japanese Cult." Pp. 96–108 in June Helm (ed.), *Essays on the Verbal and Visual Arts*. Seattle: University of Washington Press, 1968.

———"Where the Family of God Is the Family: The Role of the Dead in Japanese Households," *American Anthropologist*, LXVI (April, 1964), 300–17.

Ross, Floyd. *Shinto: The Way of Japan*. Boston, Mass.: Beacon Press, 1965

Saunders, E. Dale. *Buddhism in Japan*. Philadelphia: University of Pennsylvania Press, 1964.

Smith, Robert, and R. K. Beardsley (eds.). *Japanese Culture: Its Development and Characteristics*. Chicago, Ill.: Aldine Publishing Company, 1963.

Smith, Warren, Jr. *Confucianism in Modern Japan*. Tokyo: Hokuseido Press, 1959.

Suetsuna, Joichi, *et al. Nihonjin no Kokuminsei*. Tōkyō: Shiseidō, 1961.

Tokoro, Shigemoto. *Nichiren to Iu Hito*. Tōkyō: Shiseidō, 1966.

Tsunoda, Ryusaku, *et al.* (comps.). *Sources of Japanese Tradition*. New York: Columbia University Press, 1958.

Wright, Arthur, and Denis Twitchett (eds.). *Confucian Personalities*. Stanford, Calif.: Stanford University Press, 1962.

Selected Works on the Sociology and Psychology of Religion

Aberle, David. "A Note on the Relative Deprivation Theory as Applied to Millenarian and other Cult Movements." Pp. 537–

41 in William Lessa and Evan Vogt (eds.), *Reader in Comparative Religion*. New York: Harper and Row, 1965.

Allport, Gordon. *The Individual and His Religion*. New York: Macmillan, 1950.

———. "Religious Sentiment," *Pastoral Psychology*, VI (1955), 36–42.

Allinsmith, W. and B. "Religious Affiliation and Politico-Economic Attitude," *Public Opinion Quarterly*, XII (1948), 377–89.

Andrews, Edward Deming. *The People Called Shakers: A Search for the Perfect Society*. New York: Oxford University Press, 1953.

Argyle, Michael. *Religious Behaviour*. London: Routledge and Kegan Paul, 1958.

Barber, Bernard. "Acculturation and Messianic Movements," *American Sociological Review*, VI (October, 1941), 663–69.

Barclay, Harold. "The Plain People of Oregon," *Review of Religious Research*, VII (September, 1967), 140–65.

Becker, Howard. "Sacred and Secular Societies, Considered with Reference to Folk-State and Similar Classifications," *Social Forces*, XXVIII (May, 1950), 361–76.

Bender, Irving. "Changes in Religious Interest: A Retest after Fifteen Years," *Journal of Abnormal and Social Psychology*, LVII (July, 1958), 41–46.

Benson, Purnell. *Religion in Contemporary Culture: A Study of Religion Through Social Science*. New York: Harper, 1960.

Berger, Peter. "Sectarianism and Religious Sociation," *American Journal of Sociology*, LXIV (July, 1958), 41–44.

———. "The Sociological Study of Sectarianism," *Social Research*, XXI (Winter, 1954), 467–85.

Bittner, Egon. "Radicalism and the Organization of Radical Movements," *American Sociological Review*, XXVIII (December, 1963), 928–40.

Boisen, Anton. "The Development and Validation of Religious Faith," *Psychiatry*, XIV (1951), 455–62.

Braden, Charles. "The Study of Spiritual Healing in the Churches," *Pastoral Psychology*, V (May, 1954), 9–15.

———. *They Also Believe*. New York: Macmillan, 1960.

Bram, Joseph. "Jehovah's Witnesses and the Values of American Culture," *Transactions of the New York Academy of Science*, XIX (1956), 47–54.

Brock, Timothy. "Implications of Conversion and Magnitude of Cognitive Dissonance," *Journal for the Scientific Study of Religion*, I (Spring, 1962), 198–203.

Broen, William, "A Factor-Analytic Study of Religious Attitudes," *Journal of Abnormal and Social Psychology*, LIV (1957), 176–78.

———. "Personality Correlates of Certain Religious Attitudes," *Journal of Consulting Psychology*, XIX (1955), 64.

Brothers, Joan (ed.). *Readings in the Sociology of Religion*. New York: Pergamon Press, 1967.

Brown, David, and W. L. Lowe. "Religious Beliefs and Personality Characteristics of College Students," *Journal of Social Psychology*, XXXIII (1951), 103–29.

Burchinal, Lee. "Marital Satisfaction and Religious Behavior," *American Sociological Review*, XXII (1957), 306–10.

———. "Some Social Status Criteria and Church Membership and Church Attendance, *Journal of Social Psychology*, XLIX (1959), 53–64.

Cain, Leonard, Jr. "Japanese-American Protestants: Acculturation and Assimilation," *Review of Religious Research*, III (Winter, 1962), 113–21.

Cantril, Hadley. "Educational and Economic Compositions of Religious Groups," *American Journal of Sociology*, XLIX (1943), 574–79.

Carey, Raymond, "Religion and Happiness in Marriage," *Review of Religious Research*, VII (Winter, 1967), 104–12.

Catton, William, Jr. "What Kind of People Does a Religious Cult Attract?" *American Sociological Review*, XXII (October, 1957), 561–66.

Clark, Elmer. *The Psychology of Religious Awakening*. New York: Macmillan, 1929.

———. *The Small Sects in America*. Nashville, Tenn.: Abingdon-Cokesbury, 1949.

Clark, Walter. *The Oxford Group*. New York: Bookman Associates, 1951.

———. *The Psychology of Religion*. New York: Macmillan, 1958.

Clear, Val. "The Church of God: A Study in Social Adaptation," *Review of Religious Research*, II (Winter, 1961), 129–33.

Cohen, Oscar. "Implications of Intergroup Relations for Research," *Review of Religious Research*, IV (Fall, 1962), 17–24.

Cohn, Norman. *The Pursuit of the Millennium*. London: Secker and Warburg, 1957.

Cohn, Werner. "Jehovah's Witnesses as a Proletarian Movement," *American Scholar*, XXIV (Summer, 1955), 281–98.

Coughenour, C. Milton. "An Application of Scale Analysis to the

Study of Religious Groups," *Rural Sociology*, XX (September-December, 1955), 197–207.

Davies, J. Kenneth, "The Mormon Church: Its Middle-Class Propensities," *Review of Religious Research*, IV (Winter, 1963), 84–95.

Demerath, Nicholas, III. "Social Stratification and Church Involvement: The Church-Sect Distinction Applied to Individual Participation," *Review of Religious Research*, II (Spring, 1961), 146–54.

Dohrman, H. T. *California Cult: The Story of "Mankind United."* Boston, Mass.: Beacon Press, 1958.

Dreger, Ralph. *Some Personality Correlates of Religious Attitudes as Determined by Projective Techniques.* (Psychological Monographs, No. 335, 1952.)

Dynes, Russell. "Church-Sect Typology and Socio-Economic Status," *American Sociological Review*, XX (1955), 555–60.

———. "The Consequences of Sectarianism for Social Participation," *Social Forces*, XXXV (May, 1957), 331–33.

———. "Rurality, Migration, and Sectarianism," *Rural Sociology*, XXI (1956), 25–28.

Eister, Allan. *Drawing Room Conversion: A Sociological Account of the Oxford Group.* Durham, N.C.: Duke University Press, 1950.

———. "Empirical Research on Religion and Society," *Review of Religious Research*, VI (Spring, 1965), 125–30.

———. "Religious Institutions in Complex Societies: Difficulties in the Theoretic Specification of Functionalism," *American Sociological Review*, XXII (August, 1957), 387–91.

Elinson, Howard. "The Implications of Pentecostal Religion for Intellectualism, Politics, and Race Relations," *American Journal of Sociology*, LXX (January, 1965), 403–15.

Elkind, David. "Age Changes in the Meaning of Religious Identity," *Review of Religious Research*, VI (Fall, 1964), 36–40.

England, R. W. "Some Aspects of Christian Science as Reflected in Letters of Testimony," *American Journal of Sociology*, LIX (March, 1954), 448–53.

Erskine, Hazel Gaudet (comp.). "The Polls: Church Attendance; Personal Religious Beliefs; Organized Religion," *Public Opinion Quarterly*, Vol. XXIX (Winter, Spring, and Summer, 1959).

Eissen-Udom, E. U. *Black Nationalism: A Search for an Identity in America.* New York: Dell, 1964.

Faulkner, Joseph, and Gordon De Jong, "Religiosity in 5-D: An

Empirical Analysis," *Social Forces*, XLV (December, 1966), 246–54.

Festinger, Leon. *When Prophecy Fails*. Minneapolis: University of Minnesota Press, 1956.

Firey, Walter. "Informal Organization and the Theory of Schism," *American Sociological Review*, XII (February, 1948), 15–24.

Ford, Thomas. "Religious Thought and Beliefs in the Southern Appalachians as Revealed by an Attitude Survey," *Review of Religious Research*, III (Summer, 1961), 2–21.

———. "Status, Residence, and Fundamentalist Religious Beliefs in the Southern Appalachians," *Social Forces*, XXXIX (October, 1960), 41–49.

Francis, E. K. *In Search of Utopia: The Mennonites in Manitoba*. Glencoe, Ill.: Free Press, 1955.

———. "Toward a Typology of Religious Orders," *American Journal of Sociology*, LV (1950), 437–49.

Frerking, Ken. "Religious Participation of Lutheran Students, *Review of Religious Research*, VI (Spring, 1965), 153–62.

Frymier, Jack. "Relationship Between Church Attendance and Authoritarianism," *Religious Education*, LIV (July-August, 1959), 369–71.

Fukuyama, Yoshio. "Functional Analysis of Religious Beliefs," *Religious Education*, LVI (November-December, 1961), 446–51.

———. "The Major Dimensions of Church Membership," *Review of Religious Research*, II (Spring, 1961), 154–61.

George, Katherine and Charles. "Roman Catholic Sainthood and Social Status: A Statistical and Analytical Study," *Journal of Religion*, XXXV (Spring, 1955), 85–98.

Glenn, Norval, and Ruth Hyland. "Religious Preferences and Worldly Success: Some Evidence from National Surveys," *American Sociological Review*, XXXII (February, 1967), 73–85.

Glock, Charles. "On the Study of Religious Commitment," *Religious Education*, LVII (July–August, 1962), S-98—S-110.

———. "Religion and the Integration of Society," *Review of Religious Research*, II (Fall, 1960), 49–61.

———, and Rodney Stark. *Christian Beliefs and Anti-Semitism*. New York: Harper and Row, 1966.

———, and Rodney Stark. *Religion and Society in Tension*. Chicago, Ill.: Rand McNally, 1965.

———, and Benjamin Ringer. "Church Policy and Attitudes of Ministers and Parishioners on Social Issues," *American Sociological Review*, XXI (April, 1956), 148–55.

————, Benjamin Ringer, and Earle Bobbie. *To Comfort and to Challenge: A Dilemma of the Contemporary Church.* Los Angeles: University of California Press, 1967.

Grafton, Thomas. "God in the Personality Paradigm," *Review of Religious Research,* V (Fall, 1963), 21–29.

Griswold, Alfred Whitney. "New Thought: A Cult of Success, *"American Journal of Sociology,* XL (November, 1934), 309–18.

Hammond, Phillip. "Contemporary Protestant Ideology: A Typology of Church Images," *Review of Religious Research,* II (Spring, 1961), 161–69.

————. "The Migrating Sect: An Illustration From Early Norwegian Immigration," *Social Forces,* XLI (March, 1963), 275–83.

Harms, Ernest. "Ethical and Psychological Implications of Religious Conversion," *Review of Religious Research,* III (Winter, 1962), 122–31.

————. "Religious Conversion, Mental Health, and Priestly Responsibility," *Religious Education,* LIV (May–June, 1959), 217–22.

Hawthorn, Harry. "A Test of Simmel on the Secret Society: The Doukhobors of British Columbia," *American Journal of Sociology,* LXII (July, 1956), 1–7.

————. *The Doukhobors of British Columbia.* Vancouver, B.C.: University of British Columbia, 1955.

Hill, William. "The Psychology of Conversion," *Pastoral Psychology,* VI (1955), 43–46.

Hiltner, Seward, and William Rogers. "Research on Religion and Personality Dynamics," *Religious Education,* LVII (July–August, 1962), S-128—S-140.

Hoekema, Anthony. *The Four Major Cults.* Grand Rapids, Mich.: William B. Eerdmans, 1963.

Holt, John. "Holiness Religion: Cultural Shock and Social Reorganization," *American Sociological Review,* V (October, 1940), 740–47.

Hoult, Thomas. "A Functional Theory of Religion," *Sociology and Social Research,* XLI (March, 1957), 277–80.

————. *The Sociology of Religion.* New York: Dryden, 1958.

Houser, Frank. "The Structure and Institutionalization of a Protest Group," *Illinois Academy of Science Transactions,* XLII (1949), 130–39.

Hyde, Kenneth. "The Religious Concepts of Adolescents," *Religious Education,* LVI (September–October, 1961), 329–33.

Jackson, Allen. "Religious Beliefs and Expressions of the Southern Highlander," *Review of Religious Research*, III (Summer, 1961), 21–39.

Johnson, Benton. "A Critical Appraisal of the Church-Sect Typology," *American Sociological Review*, XXII (February, 1957), 88–92.

————. "Ascetic Protestantism and Political Preference," *Public Opinion Quarterly*, XXVI (Spring, 1962), 35–46.

————. "Ascetic Protestantism and Political Preference in the Deep South," *American Journal of Sociology*, LXIX (January, 1964), 359–66.

————. "Do Holiness Sects Socialize in Dominant Values?" *Social Forces*, XXXIX (May, 1961), 309–17.

Kirkpatrick, Clifford. *Religion and Humanitarianism* (Psychological Monographs, No. 63, 1949.)

Klausner, Samuel. "Changing Ideology of the [Religio-Psychiatric] Movement," *Review of Religious Research*, VI (Fall, 1964), 7–22.

————. *Psychiatry and Religion: A Sociological Story of the New Alliance of Ministers and Psychiatrists*. Glencoe, Ill.: Free Press, 1964.

————. "The Religio-Psychiatric Movement," *Review of Religious Research*, V (Winter, 1964), 63–74.

Kleiner, Robert, *et al.* "Mental Disorder and Status Based on Religious Affiliation," *Human Relations*, XII (August, 1959), 273–76.

Knudten, Richard (ed.). *The Sociology of Religion: An Anthology.* New York: Appleton-Century-Crofts, 1967.

Lanternari, Vittorio. *The Religions of the Oppressed: A Study of Modern Messianic Cults.* New York: Alfred A. Knopf, 1963.

Laue, James. "Contemporary Revitalization Movements in Race Relations: The 'Black Muslims,'" *Social Forces*, XLII (March, 1964), 315–23.

Lazerwitz, Bernard. "Some Factors Associated with Variations in Church Attendance," *Social Forces*, XXXIX (May, 1961), 301–9.

Lenski, Gerhard. *The Religious Factor.* Garden City, N.Y.: Doubleday, 1961.

————. "Social Correlates of Religious Interest," *American Sociological Review*, XVIII (1953), 533–44.

Lincoln, C. E. *The Black Muslims in America.* Boston, Mass.: Beacon Press, 1961.

Lofland, John, and Rodney Stark. "Becoming a World-Saver: A

Theory of Conversion to a Deviant Perspective," *American Sociological Review*, XXX (December, 1965), 862–74.

———. *Doomsday Cult*. Englewood Cliffs, N.J.: Prentice-Hall, 1966.

Lowe, Warner. "Religious Beliefs and Religious Delusions—A Comparative Study of Religious Projection," *American Journal of Psychotherapy*, IX (1955), 54–61.

Luckmann, Thomas. *The Invisible Religion: The Problem of Religion in Modern Society*. New York: Macmillan, 1967.

Main, Earl. "Participation in Protestant Churches," *Review of Religious Research*, VIII (Spring, 1967), 176–83.

Mann, William. *Sect, Cult, and Church in Alberta*. Toronto: University of Toronto Press, 1955.

Maranell, Gary. "An Examination of Some Religious and Political Attitude Correlates of Bigotry," *Social Forces*, XLV (March, 1967), 356–61.

Martin, D. A. "The Denomination," *British Journal of Sociology*, XII (March, 1962), 1–14.

Marx, Gary. "Religion: Opiate or Inspiration of Civil Rights Militancy among Negroes?" *American Sociological Review*, XXXII (February, 1967), 64–72.

Moberg, David. "Does Social Class Shape the Church?" *Review of Religious Research*, I (Winter, 1960), 110–15.

———. *The Church as a Social Institution*. Englewood Cliffs, N.J.: Prentice-Hall, 1962.

———. "Potential Uses of the Church-Sect Typology in Comparative Religious Research," *International Journal of Comparative Sociology*, II (March, 1961), 47–58.

Mueller, Samuel. "Rokeach and the Church: A Theory of Organizational Reaction Formation," *Review of Religious Research*, VIII (Spring, 1967), 131–40.

Myers, George. "Patterns of Church Distribution and Movement," *Social Forces*, XL (May, 1962), 354–60.

Nelson, M. O., and E. M. Jones. "An Application of the Q-Technique to the Study of Religious Concepts," *Psychological Reports*, III (1957), 293–97.

Niebuhr, H. Richard. *Social Sources of Denominationalism*. New York: Holt, 1929.

Nottingham, Elizabeth. *Religion and Society*. New York: Doubleday, 1954.

Oates, Wayne. *Religious Dimensions of Personality*. New York: Association Press, 1957.

———. *Religious Factors in Mental Illness.* New York: Association Press, 1955.

———. "The Role of Religion in the Psychoses," *Journal of Pastoral Care,* III, (1949), 21–30.

O'Dea, Thomas. "Mormonism and the Avoidance of Sectarian Stagnation: A Study of Church, Sect, and Incipient Nationality," *American Journal of Sociology,* LX (November, 1954), 285–93.

———. *The Mormons.* Chicago, Ill.: University of Chicago Press, 1957.

———. "Sociological Dilemmas: Five Paradoxes of Institutionalization." In Edward Tiryakian (ed.), *Sociological Theory, Values, and Sociocultural Change: Essays in Honor of Pitirim A. Sorokim.* New York: Free Press of Glencoe, 1964.

Olt, Russell. *An Approach to the Psychology of Religion.* Boston, Mass.: Christopher, 1956.

Parsons, Talcott. "The Theoretical Development of the Sociology of Religion," *Journal of the History of Ideas,* V (1944), 176–90.

Payne, Raymond. "Knowledge of the Bible Among Protestant and Jewish University Students: An Exploratory Study," *Religious Education,* LVIII (March–April, 1963), 289–93.

Perry, Everett. "Socio-Economic Factors and American Fundamentalism," *Review of Religious Research,* I (Fall, 1959), 57–61.

Pfautz, Harold. "Christian Science: A Case Study of the Social Psychological Aspects of Secularization," *Social Forces,* XXXIV (March, 1956), 246–51.

———. "The Sociology of Secularization," *American Journal of Sociology,* LXI (1955), 121–28.

Photiadis, John, and Jeanne Bigger. "Religiosity, Education, and Ethnic Distance," *American Journal of Sociology,* LXVII (1962), 666–72.

———, and A. L. Johnson. "Orthodoxy, Church Participation, and Authoritarianism," *American Journal of Sociology,* LXIX (November, 1963), 244–48.

Poit, Carl. "A Study Concerning Religious Belief and Denominational Affiliation," *Religious Education,* LVII (May–June, 1962), 214–16.

Pope, Liston. *Millhands and Preachers.* New Haven, Conn.: Yale University Press, 1942.

———. "Religion and the Class Structure," *Annals of the Ameri-*

can Academy of Social and Political Science, Whole Number 256 (1948).

Putney, Snell, and Russell Middleton. "Dimension and Correlates of Religious Ideologies," *Social Forces,* XXXIX (May, 1961), 285–90.

Redekop, Calvin. "Decision-Making in a Sect," *Review of Religious Research,* II (Fall, 1960), 79–86.

———, and John Hosteller. "Education and Boundary Maintenance in Three Ethnic Groups," *Review of Religious Research,* V (Winter, 1964), 80–91.

Rokeach, Milton. *The Open and Closed Mind.* New York: Basic Books, 1960.

Rosenblum, Abraham. "Ethnic Prejudice as Related to Social Class and Religiosity," *Sociology and Social Research,* XLIII (March–April, 1959), 272–75.

Salisbury, W. Seward. "Faith, Ritualism, Charismatic Leadership and Religious Behavior," *Social Forces,* XXXIV (March, 1956), 241–45.

———. "Religion and Secularization," *Social Forces,* XXXVI (March, 1958), 209–13.

Salzman, Leon. "The Psychology of Religious and Ideological Conversion," *Psychiatry,* XVI (1953), 177–87.

Sargent, Leslie. "Occupational Status in a Religious Group," *Review of Religious Research,* IV (Spring, 1963), 149–55.

Schall, Mason, and Jerome Beker. "A Comparison of the Religious Beliefs of Delinquent and Non-Delinquent Protestant Adolescent Boys," *Religious Education,* LIX (May–June, 1964), 250–52.

Schellenberg, James, *et al.* "Religiosity and Social Attitudes in an Urban Congregation," *Review of Religious Research,* VI (Spring, 1965), 142–46.

Schneider, Louis, and Sanford Dornbusch. *Popular Religion: Inspirational Books in America.* Chicago, Ill.: University of Chicago Press, 1958.

———. "Inspirational Religious Literature: From Latent to Manifest Functions of Religion," *American Journal of Sociology,* LXII (1957), 476–81.

Schroeder, W. Widick. "Cognitive Structures and Religious Research," *Review of Religious Research,* III (Fall, 1961), 72–81.

Skidmore, Rex. "The Protestant Church and Recreation—An Example of Social Change," *Social Forces,* XX (1942), 364–70.

Smith, Elmer Lewis. "Personality Differences Between Amish and

Non-Amish Children," *Rural Sociology*, XXIII (December, 1958), 371–76.

Southard, Samuel. "Sectarianism and Psychoses," *Religion in Life*, XXIII (Autumn, 1954), 580–90.

Spencer, Robert. "Social Structure of a Contemporary Japanese-American Buddhist Church," *Social Forces*, XX (1948), 281–87.

Spilka, Bernard, *et al.* "The Concept of God: A Factor-Analytic Study," *Review of Religious Research*, VI (Fall, 1964), 28–36.

———, and James Reynolds. "Religion and Prejudice: A Factor-Analytic Study," *Review of Religious Research*, VI (Spring, 1965), 163–68.

Spitzer, Allen and Mary. "Religious Reorganization Among the Montana Blackfeet," *Review of Religious Research*, II (Summer, 1960), 19–35.

Stanley Gordon. "Personality and Attitude Correlates of Religious Conversion," *Journal for the Scientific Study of Religion*, IV (October, 1964), 60–63.

Stroup, Herbert. *The Jehovah's Witnesses*. New York: Columbia University Press, 1945.

Strunk, Orlo, Jr. "Motivational Factors and Psychotherapeutic Aspects of a Healing Cult," *Journal of Pastoral Care*, IX (Winter, 1955), 213–30.

——— (ed.). *Readings in the Psychology of Religion*. New York: Abingdon Press, 1959.

Talmon, Yonina. "Pursuit of the Millennium: The Relation Between Religious and Social Change." Pp. 522–36 in William Lessa and Evan Vogt (eds.), *Reader in Comparative Religion*. New York: Harper and Row, 1965.

Tannenbaum, Arnold, and Jerald Backman. "Attitude Uniformity and Role in a Voluntary Organization," *Human Relations*, XIX (August, 1966), 309–22.

Toch, Hans, and Robert Anderson. "Religious Belief and Denominational Affiliation," *Religious Education*, LV (May–June, 1960), 193–200.

———. *The Social Psychology of Social Movements*. Indianapolis, Ind.: Bobbs-Merrill, 1965.

Troeltsch, Ernst. *The Social Teachings of the Christian Churches*. New York: Macmillan, 1931. See especially Volume I.

Van Dyke, Paul, III, and John Pierce-Jones. "The Psychology of Religion of Middle and Late Adolescence: A Review of Empirical Research, 1950–1960," *Religious Education*, LVIII (November–December, 1963), 529–37.

Vernon, Glenn. "An Inquiry Into the Scalability of Church Orthodoxy," *Sociology and Social Research*, XXXIX, (May–June, 1955), 324–27.

———. "Background Factors Related to Church Orthodoxy," *Social Forces*, XXXIV (March, 1956), 252–54.

———. *Sociology of Religion*. New York: McGraw-Hill, 1962.

———. "Measuring Religion: Two Methods Compared," *Review of Religious Research*, III (Spring, 1962), 159–65.

Wach, Joachim. *Church, Denomination, Sect*. Evanston, Ill.: Seabury-Western Theological Seminary, 1946.

———. *Sociology of Religion*. Chicago, Ill.: University of Chicago Press, 1944.

Wallace, Anthony. *Religion: An Anthropological View*. New York: Random House, 1966.

———. "Revitalization Movements," *American Anthropologist*, LVIII (April, 1956), 264–81.

Wallin, Paul, "Religiosity, Sexual Gratification, and Marital Satisfaction," *American Sociological Review*, XXII (1957), 300–5.

Weatherhead, Leslie. *Psychology, Religion and Healing*. London: Hodder and Stoughton, 1951.

Weber, Max. *The Protestant Ethic and the Spirit of Capitalism*. Translated by Talcott Parsons. New York: Charles Scribners' Sons, 1958.

Weininger, Benjamin. "The Interpersonal Factor in the Religious Experience," *Psychoanalysis*, III (1955), 27–44.

Weise, Leopold von, and Howard Becker. *Systematic Sociology*. New York: John Wiley and Sons, 1932. See especially pp. 624–42, "Four Types of Religious Organization."

Whalley, Elsa. "Religion and Suicide," *Review of Religious Research*, V (Winter, 1964), 91–110.

Whitarn, Frederick. "Subdimensions of Religiosity and Race Prejudice," *Review of Religious Research*, III (Spring, 1962), 166–74.

Wiedeman, George. "The Importance of Religious Sectarianism in Psychiatric Case Study," *American Journal of Psychotherapy*, III (1949), 392–98.

Williams, Robin. "Religion, Value-Orientation, and Intergroup Conflict," *Journal of Social Issues*, XII (1956), 12–20.

Wilson, Bryan. "An Analysis of Sect Development," *American Sociological Review*, XXIV (February, 1959), 3–15.

———. *Religion in Secular Society: A Sociological Comment*. London: C. A. Walts, 1966.

————. *Sects and Society: The Sociology of Three Religious Groups in Britain*. London: William Heinemann, 1961.

Wright, John. "Personal Adjustment and Its Relation to Religious Attitudes and Certainty," *Religious Education*, LIV (November–December, 1959), 521–23.

Yinger, J. Milton. "Problems of Integration and Pluralism Among the Privileged," *Review of Religious Research*, IV (Spring, 1963), 129–48.

————. "Religion and Social Change: Functions and Dysfunctions of Sects and Cults Among the Disprivileged," *Review of Religious Research*, IV (Winter, 1962), 65–84.

————. *Religion in the Struggle for Power*. Durham, N. C.: Duke University Press, 1946.

————. *Religion, Society and the Individual*. New York: Macmillan, 1957.

Young, Frank. "Adaptation and Pattern Integration of a California Sect," *Review of Religious Research*, I (Spring, 1960), 137–50.

Zetterberg, Hans. "The Religious Conversion as a Change of Social Roles," *Sociology and Social Research*, XXXVI (January, 1952), 159–66.

Zubek, John. "The Doukhobors: A Genetic Study on Attitudes," *Journal of Social Psychology*, XXXVI (November, 1952), 223–39.